THIS BOOK BELONGS TO:

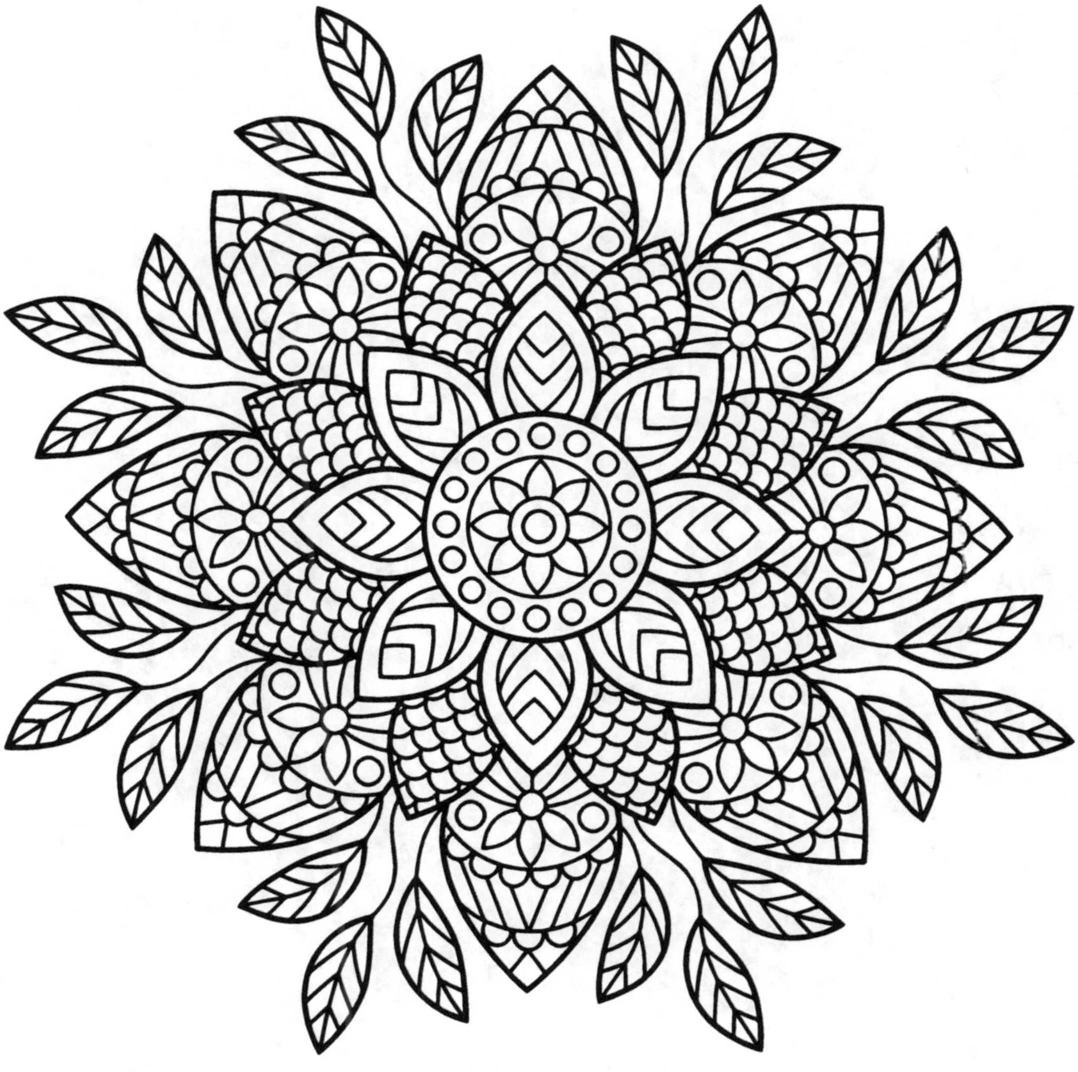

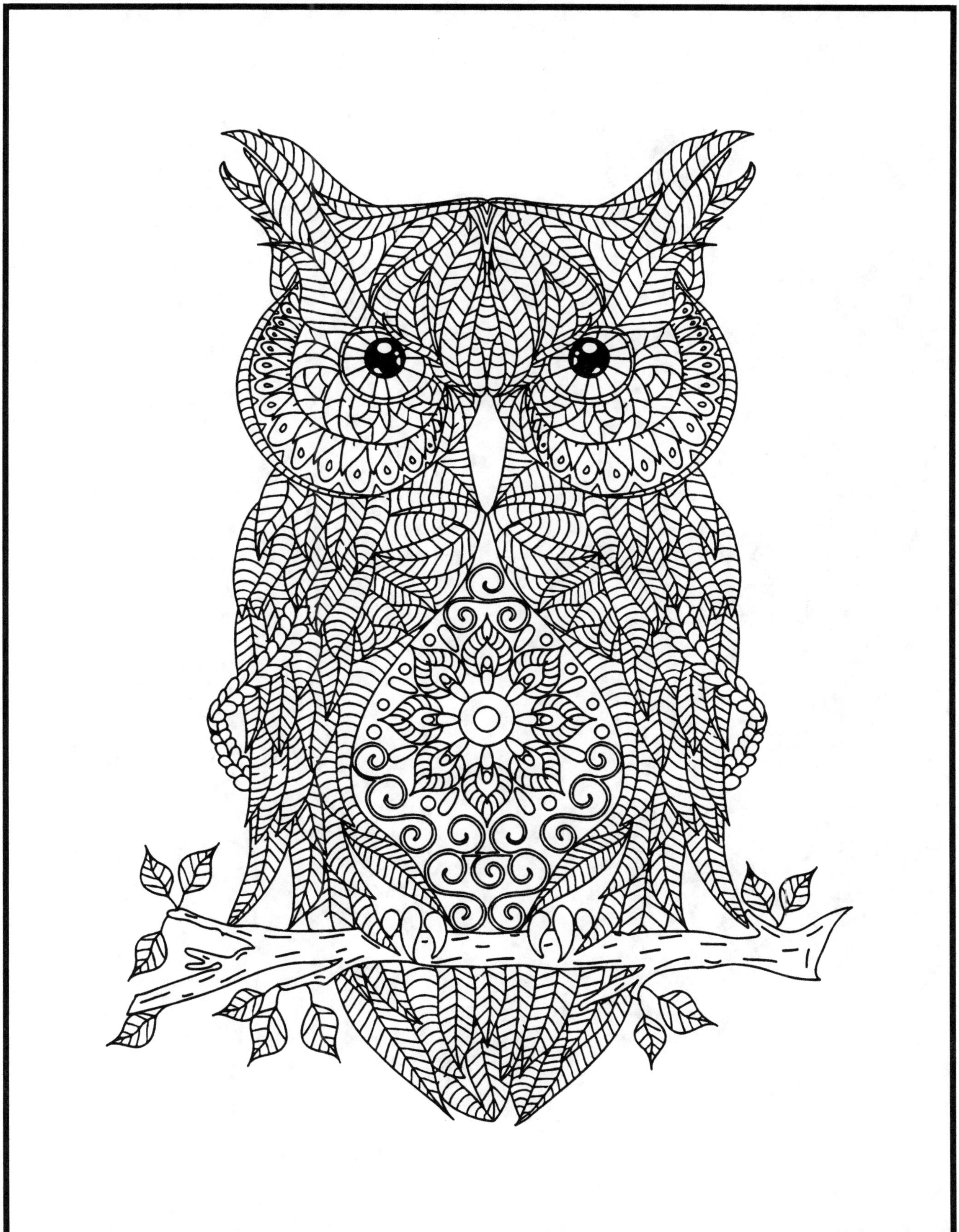

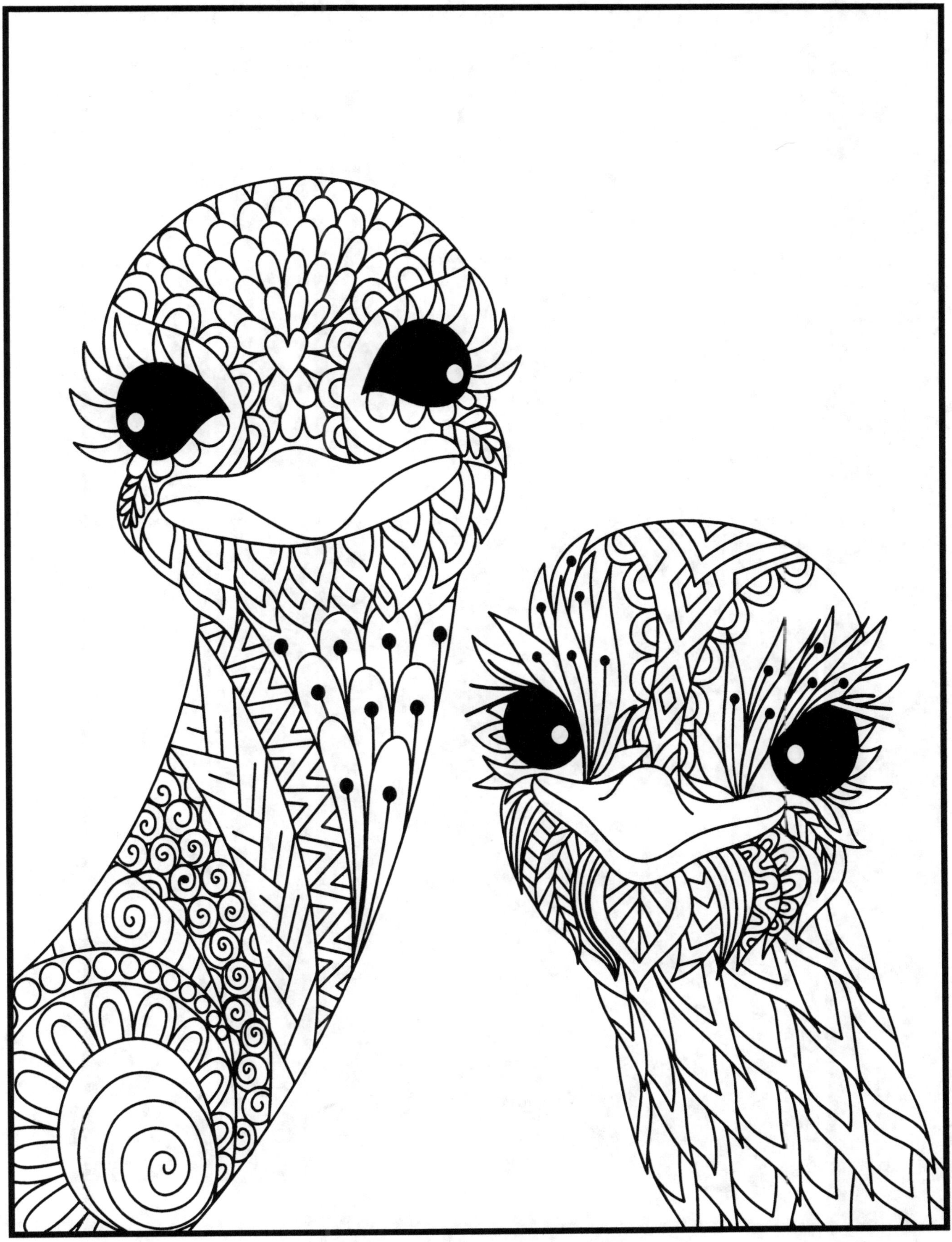

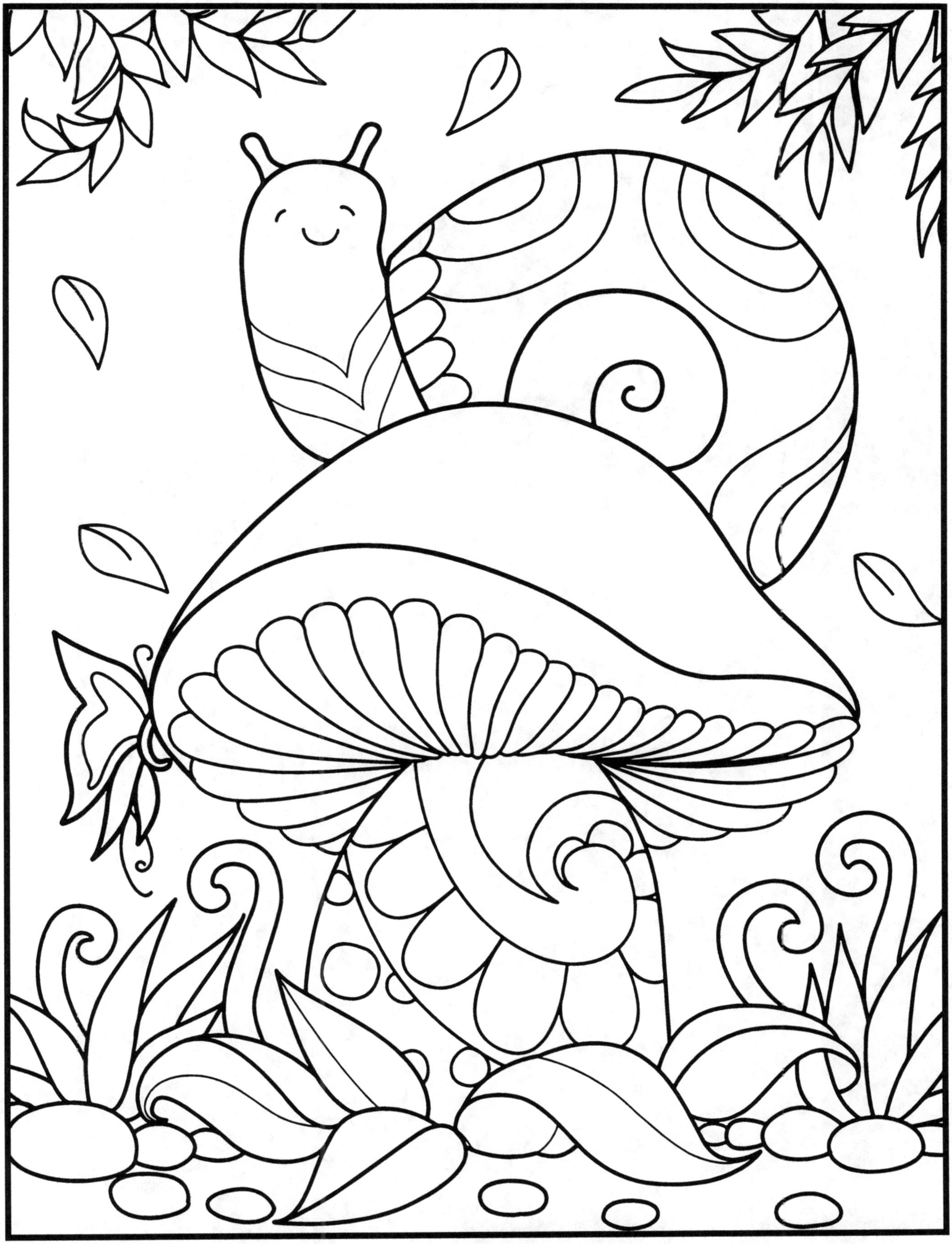

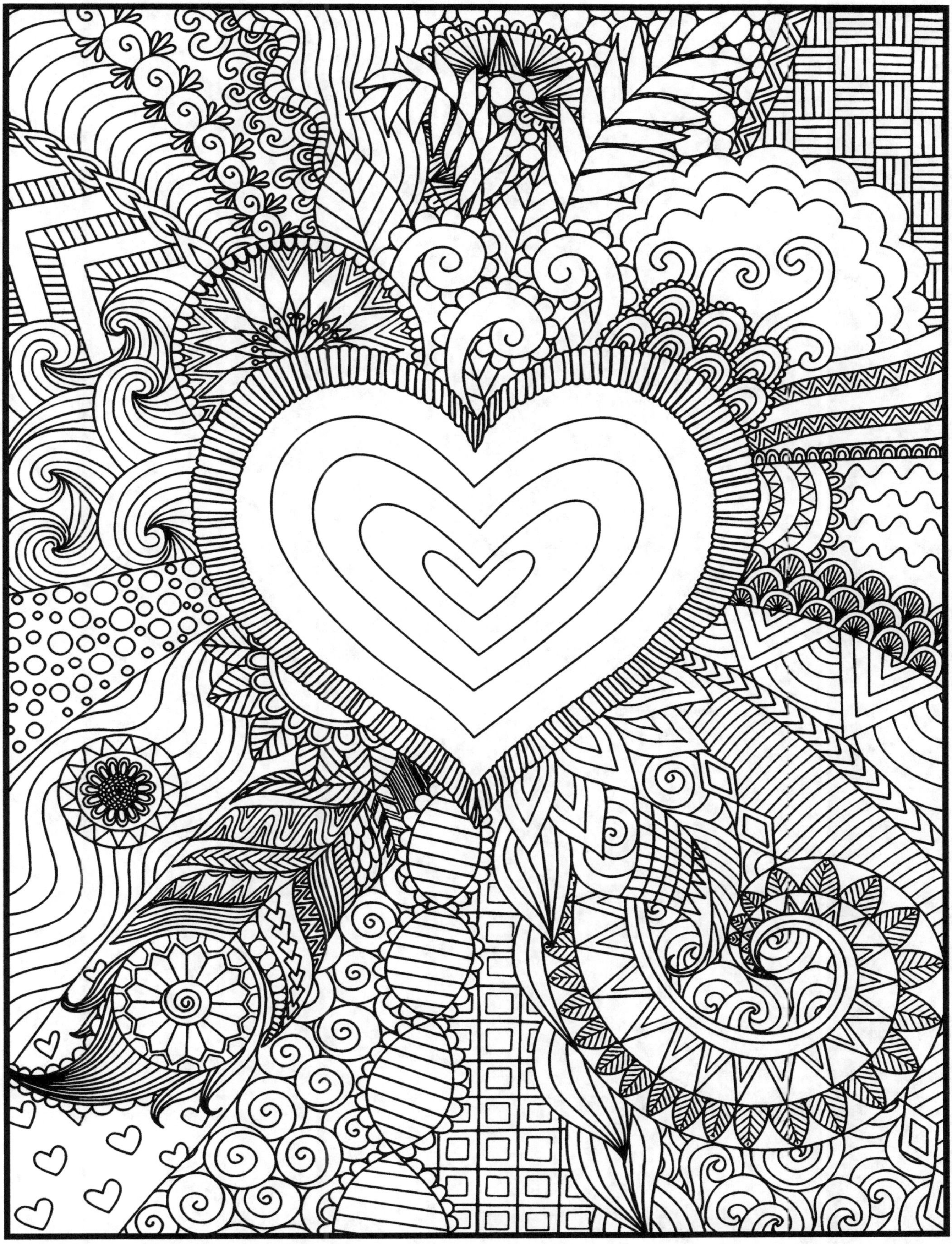

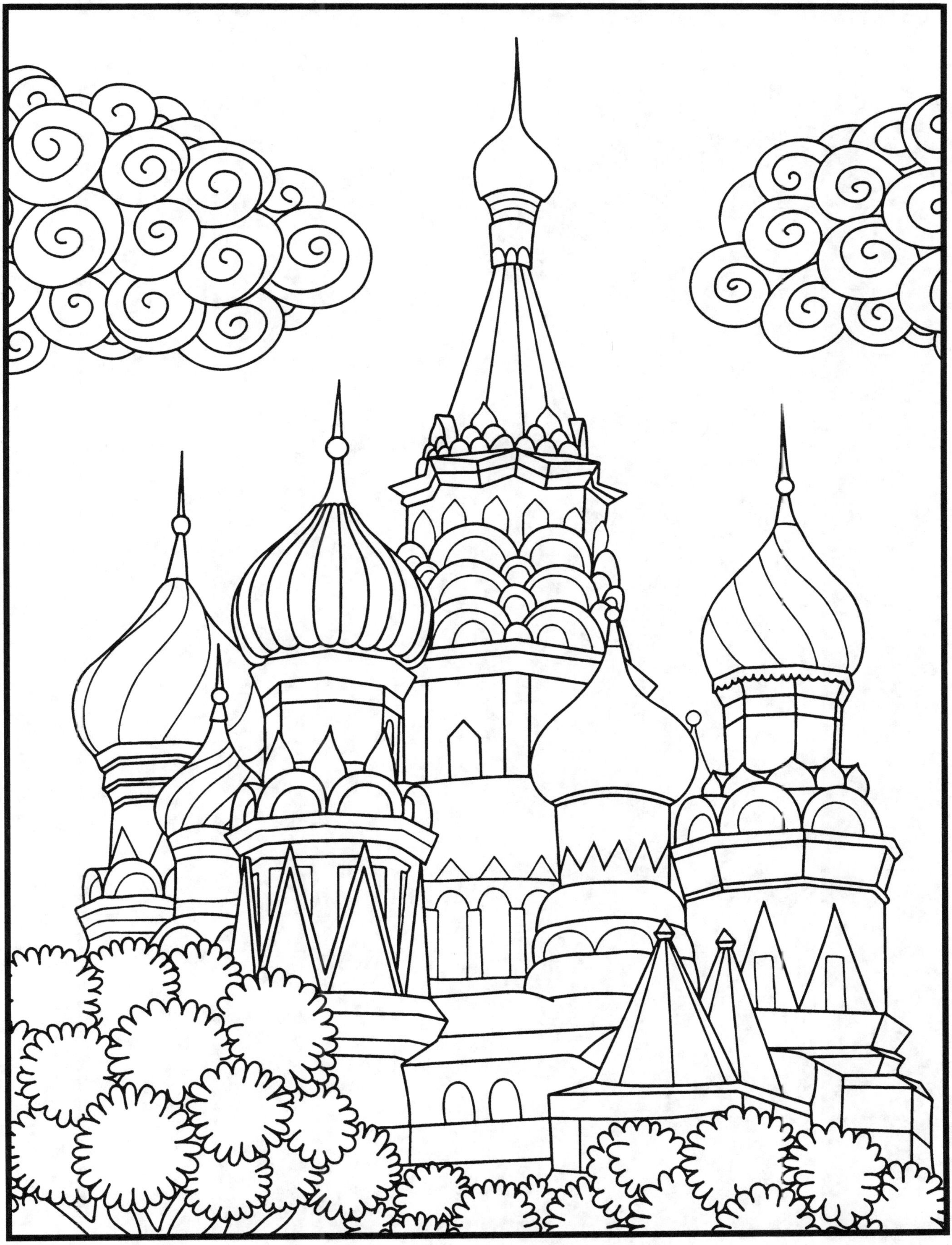

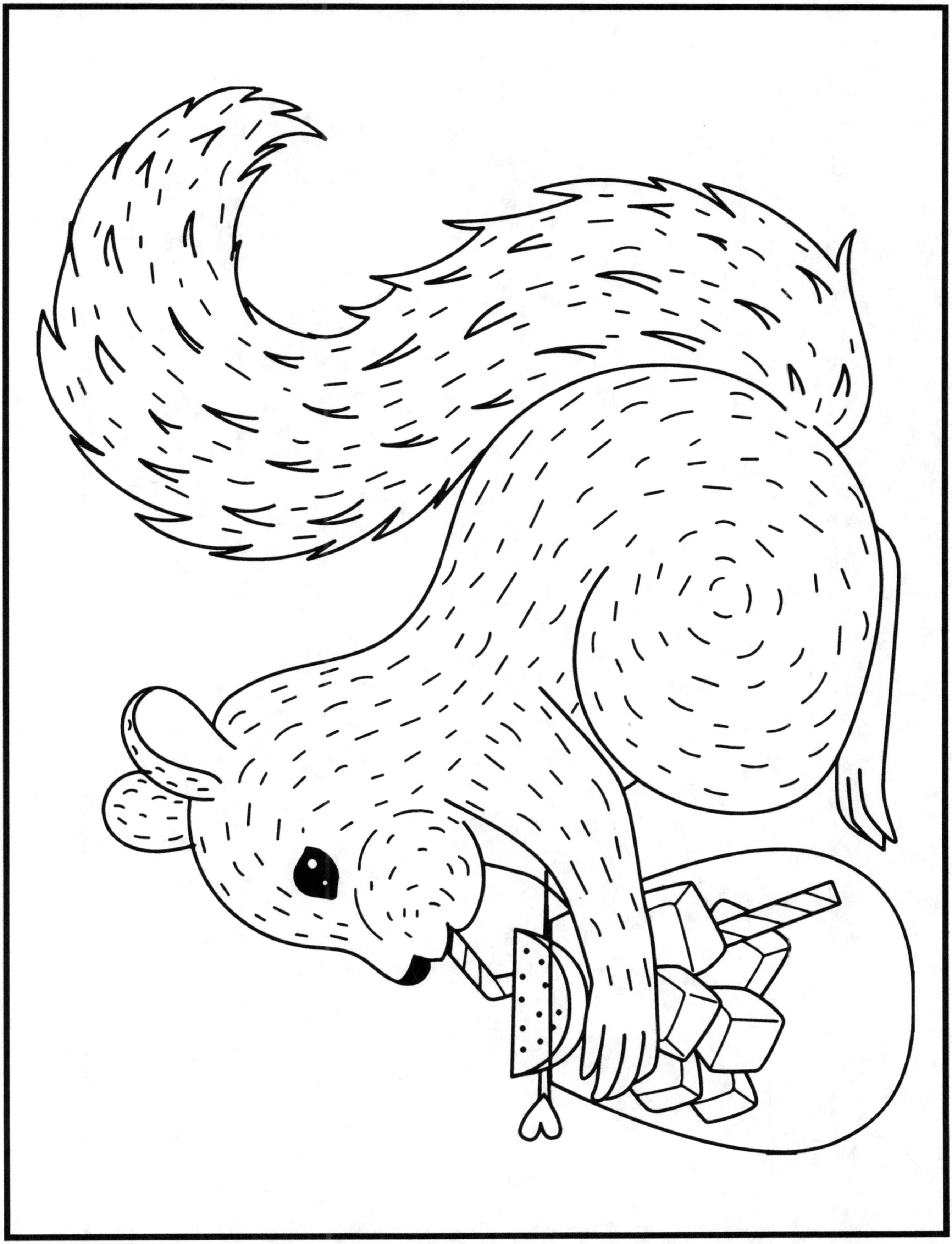

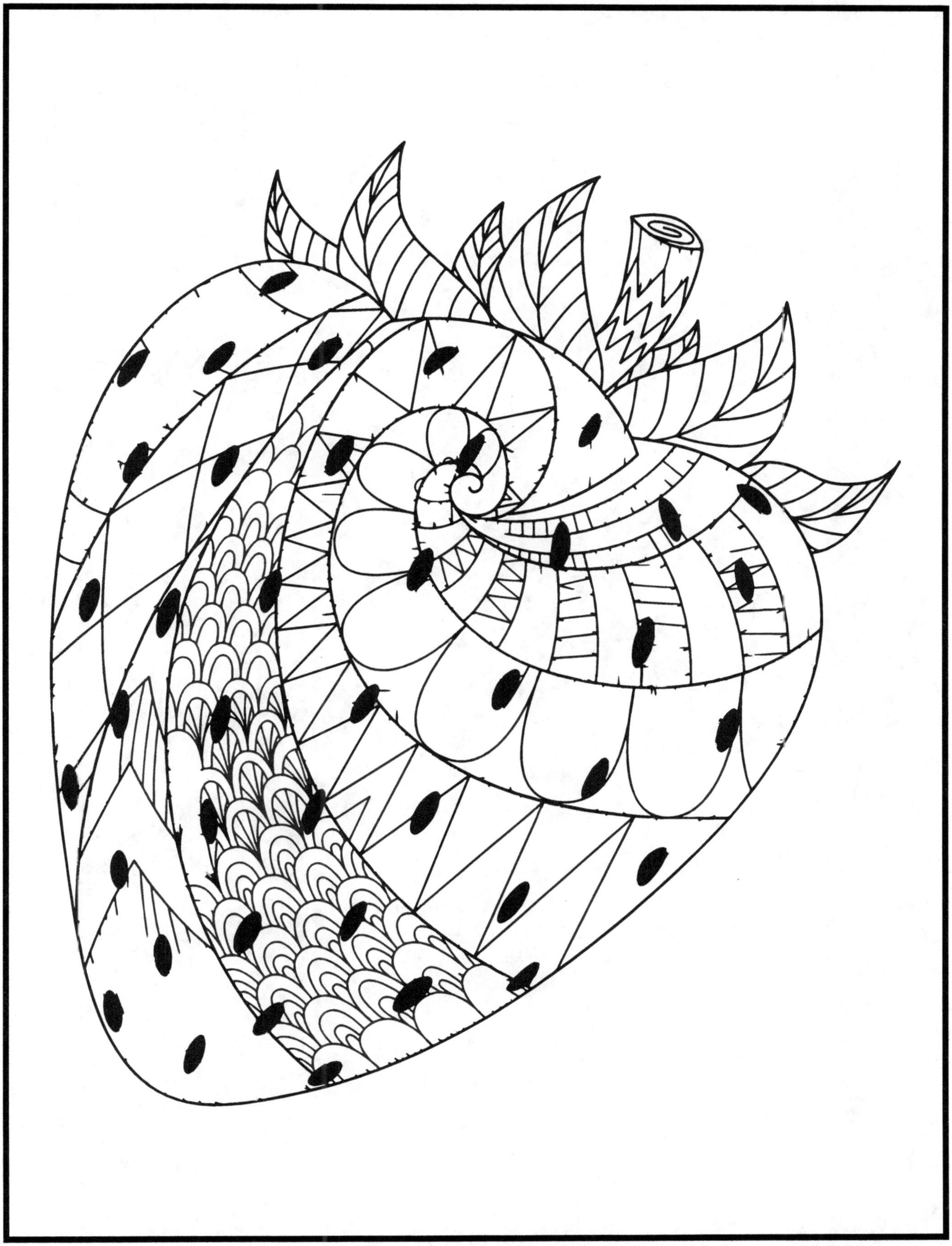

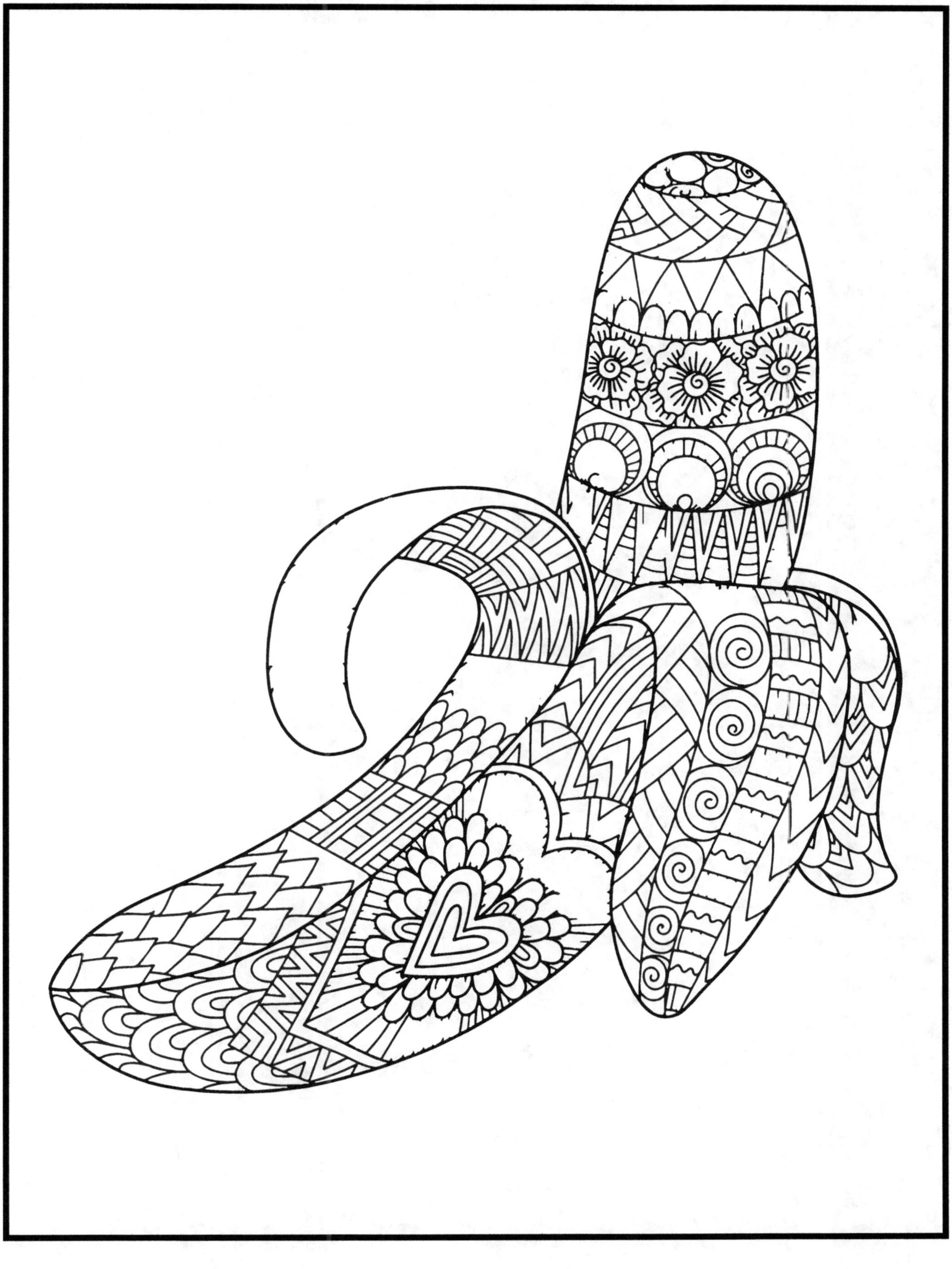

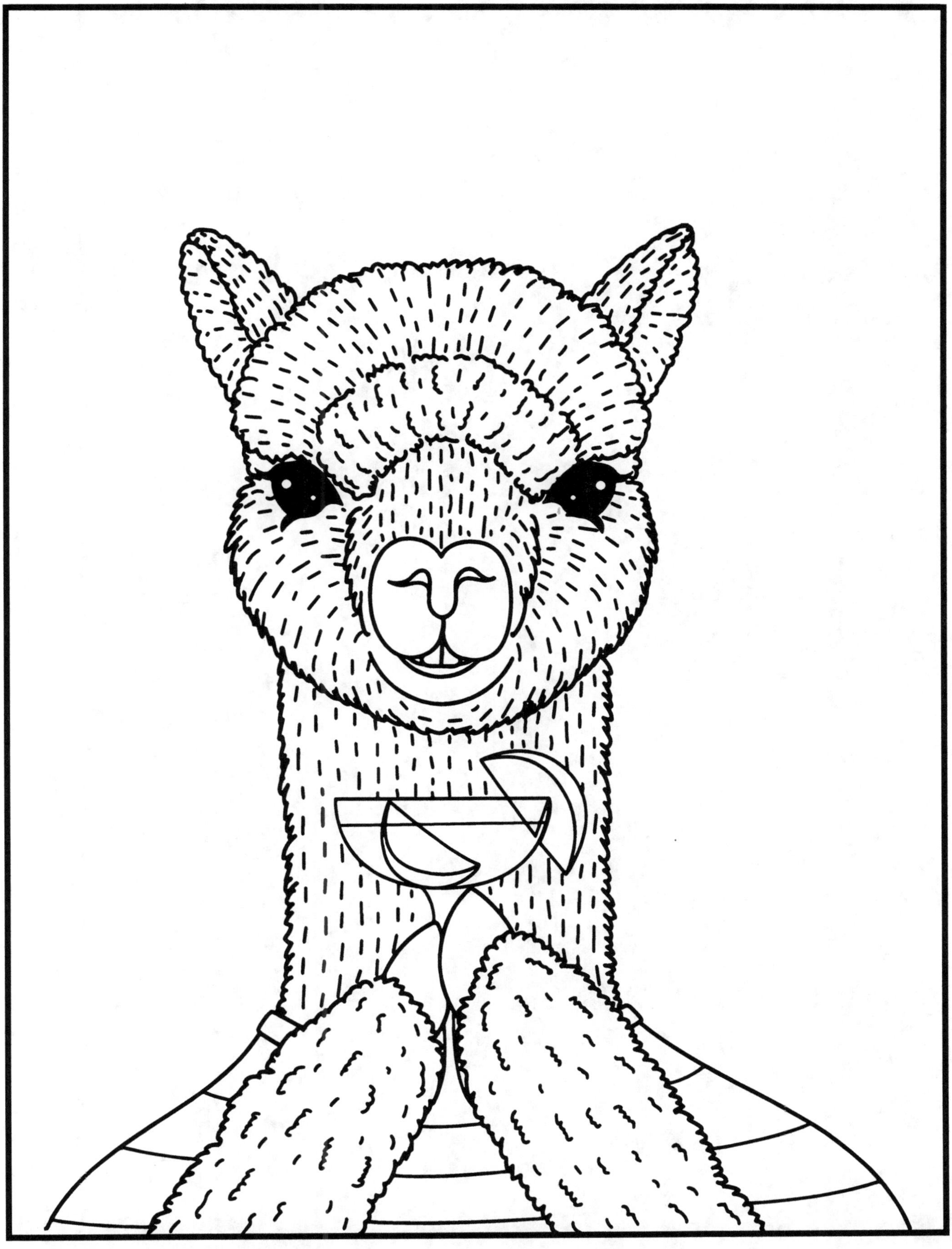

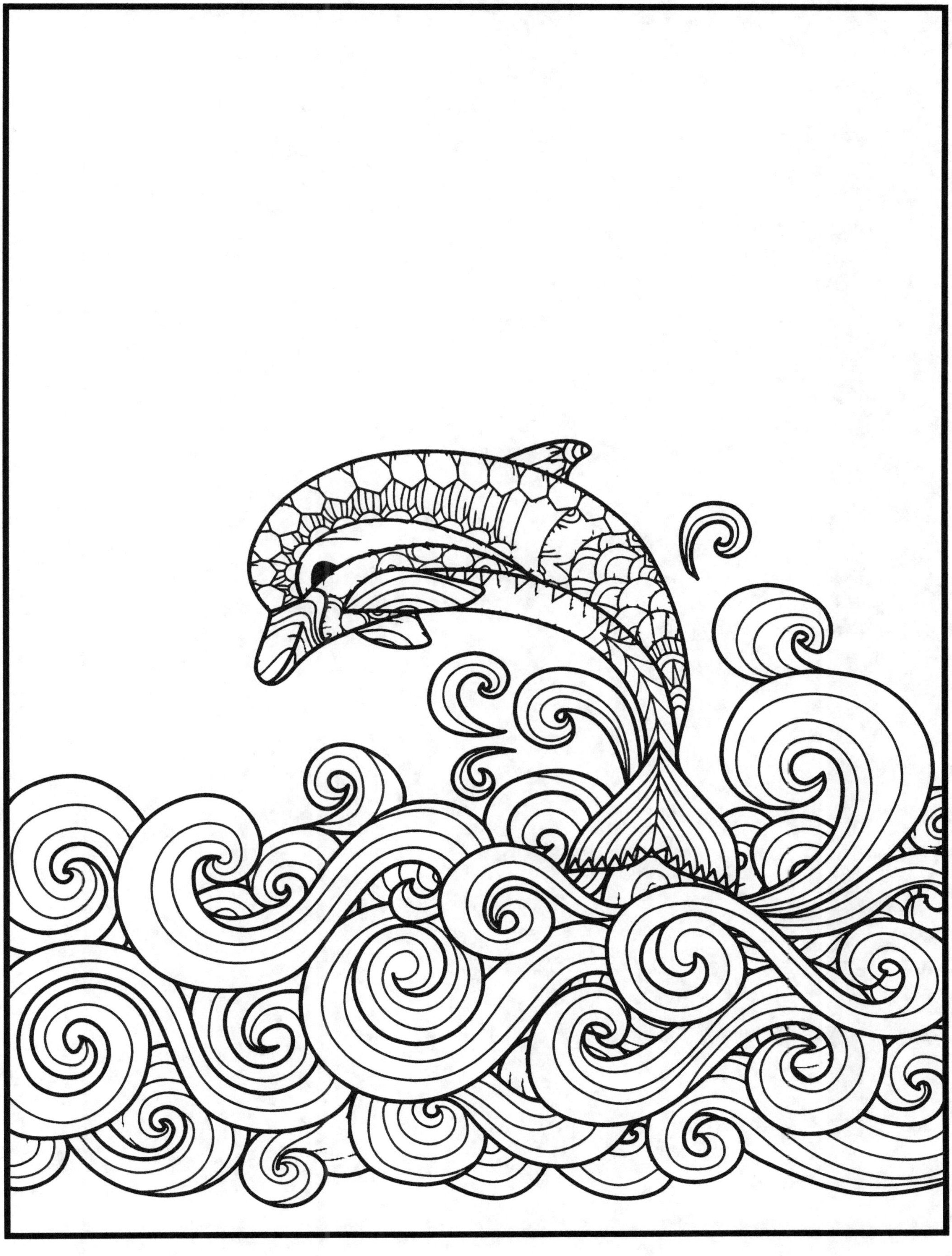

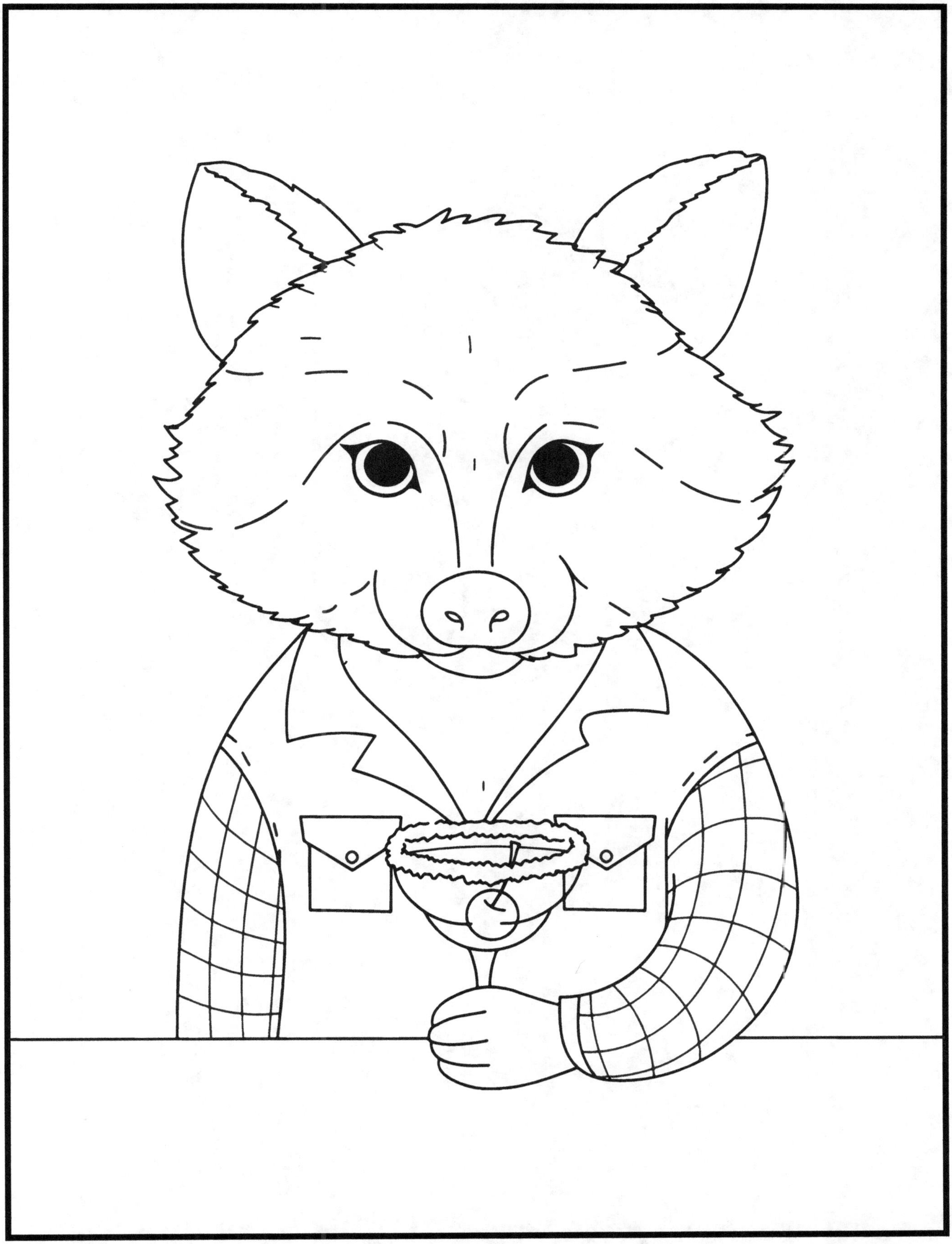

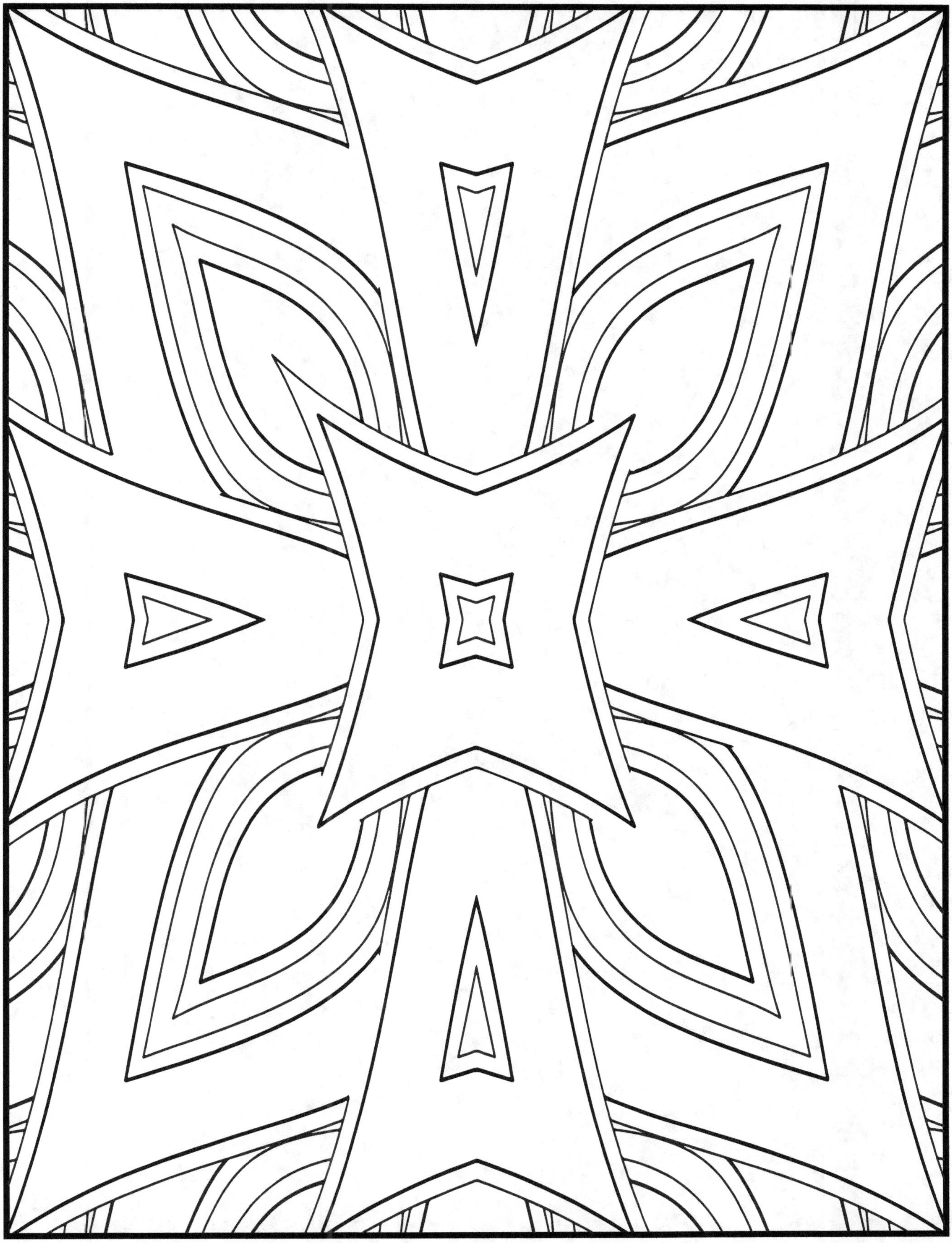

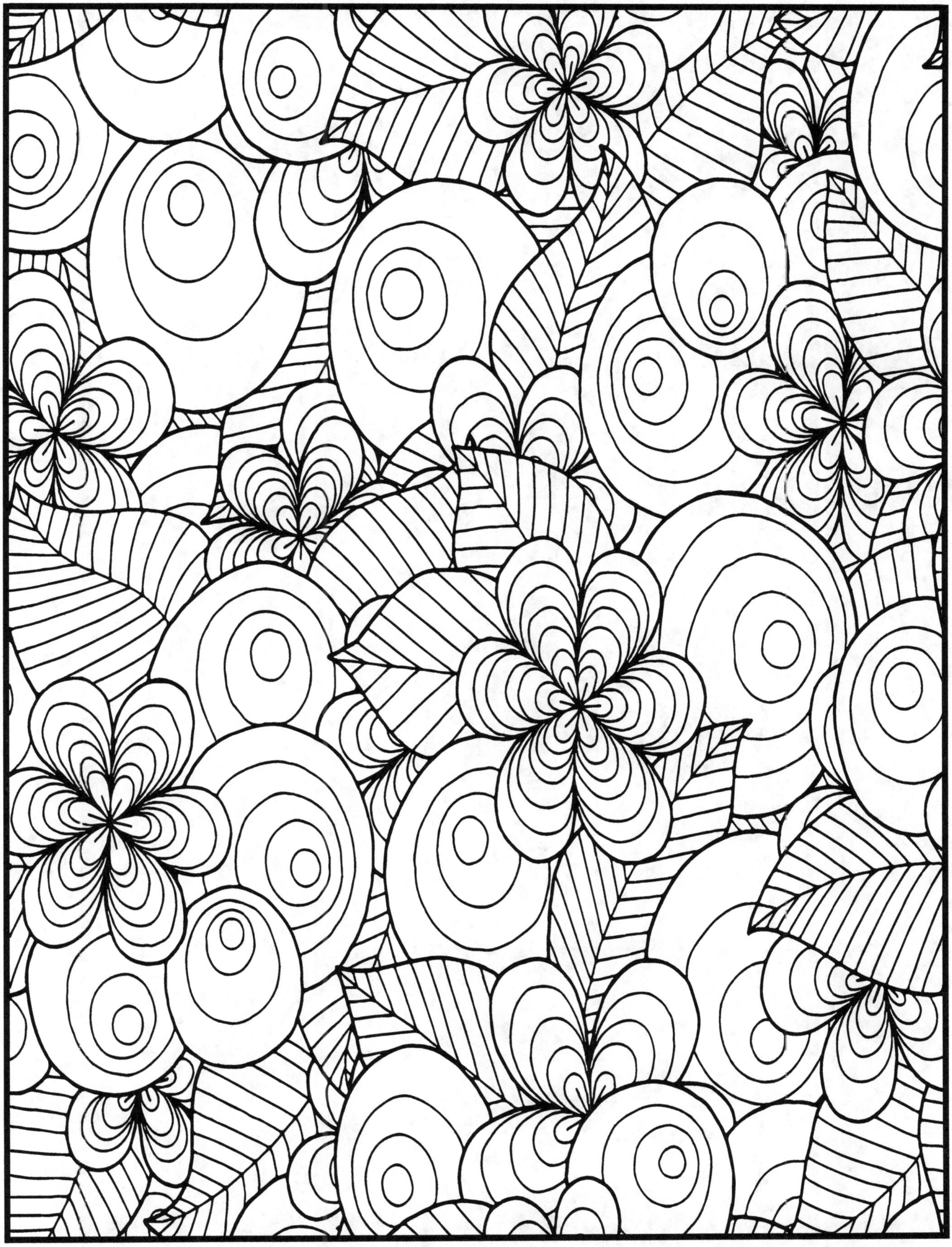

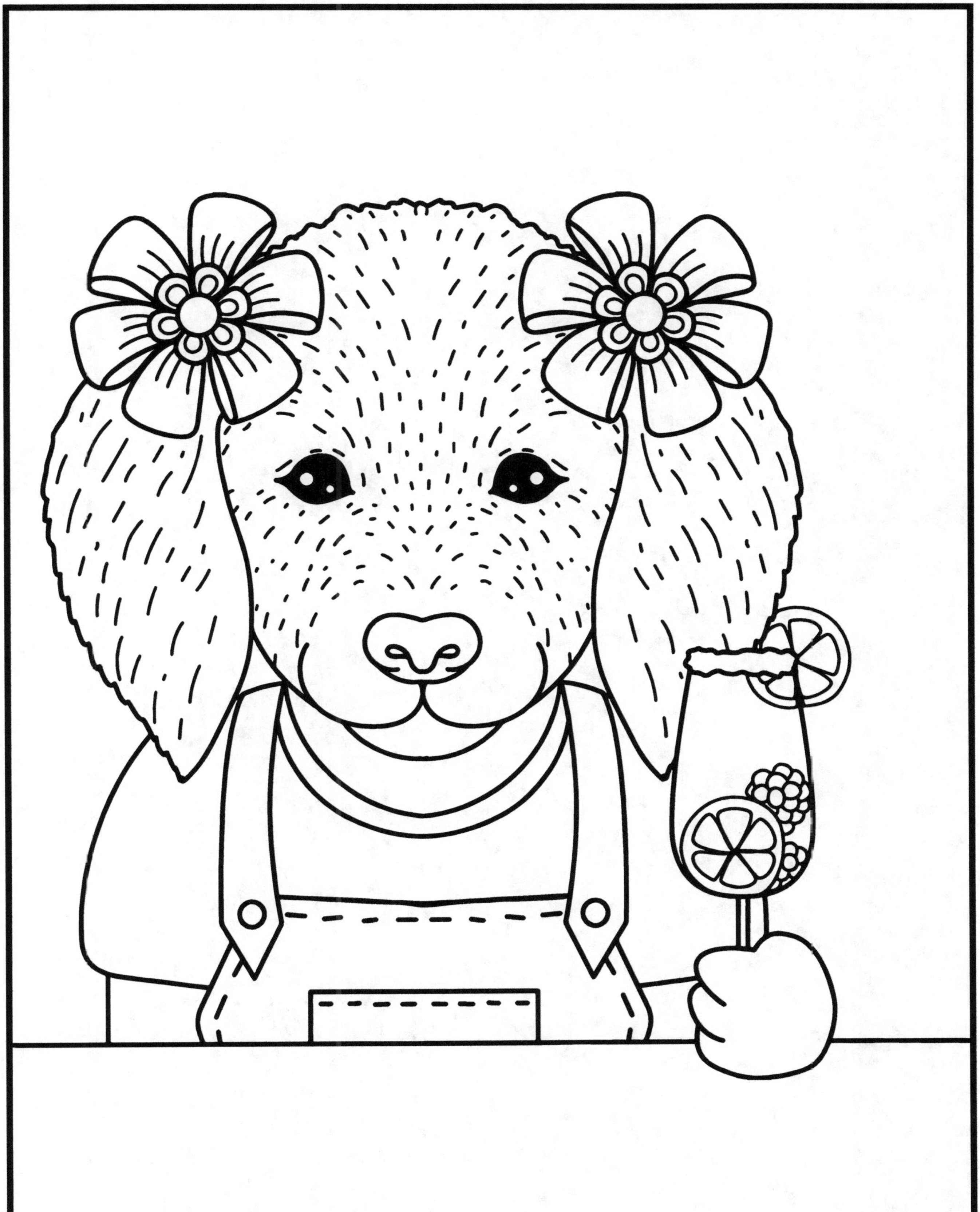

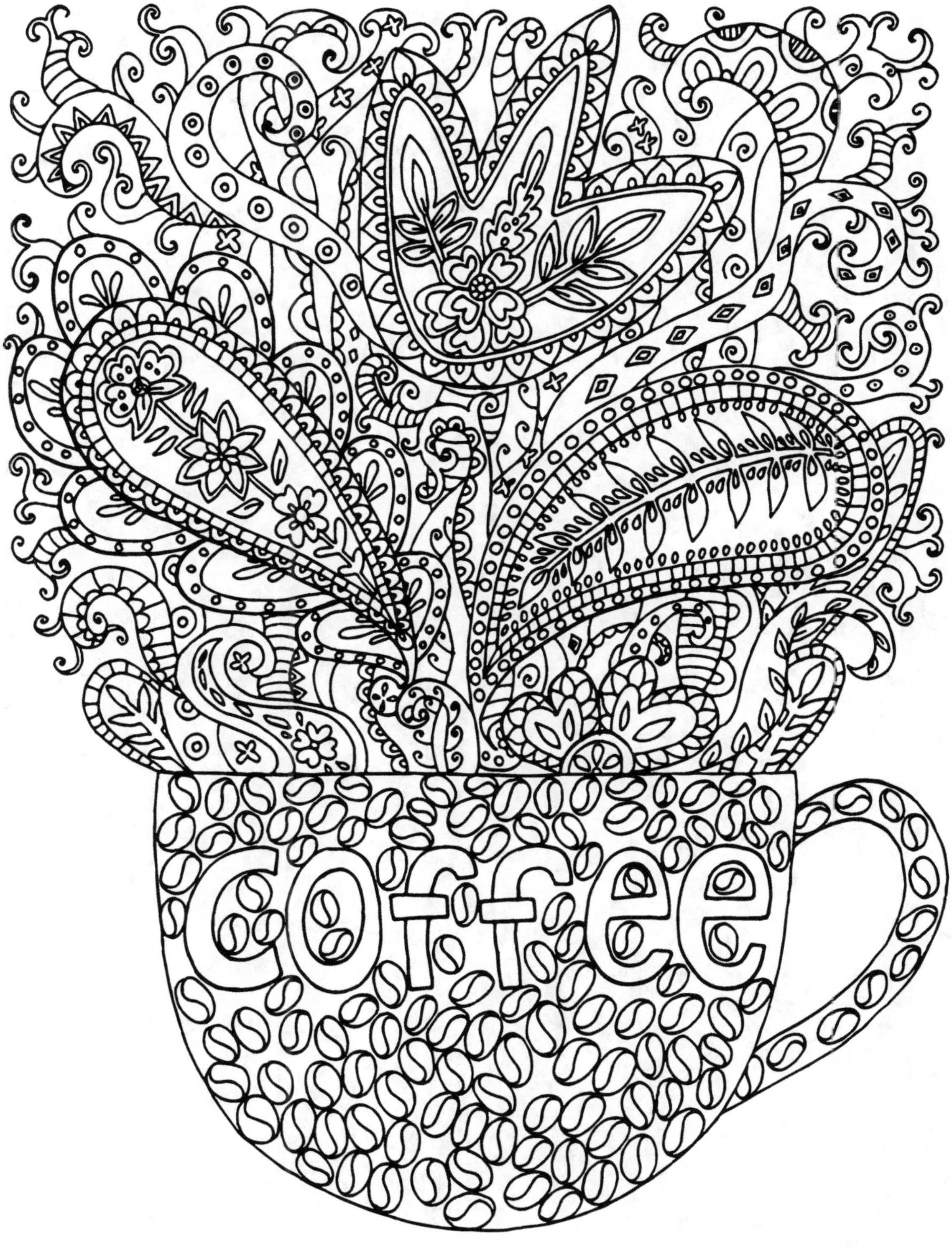
Coffee

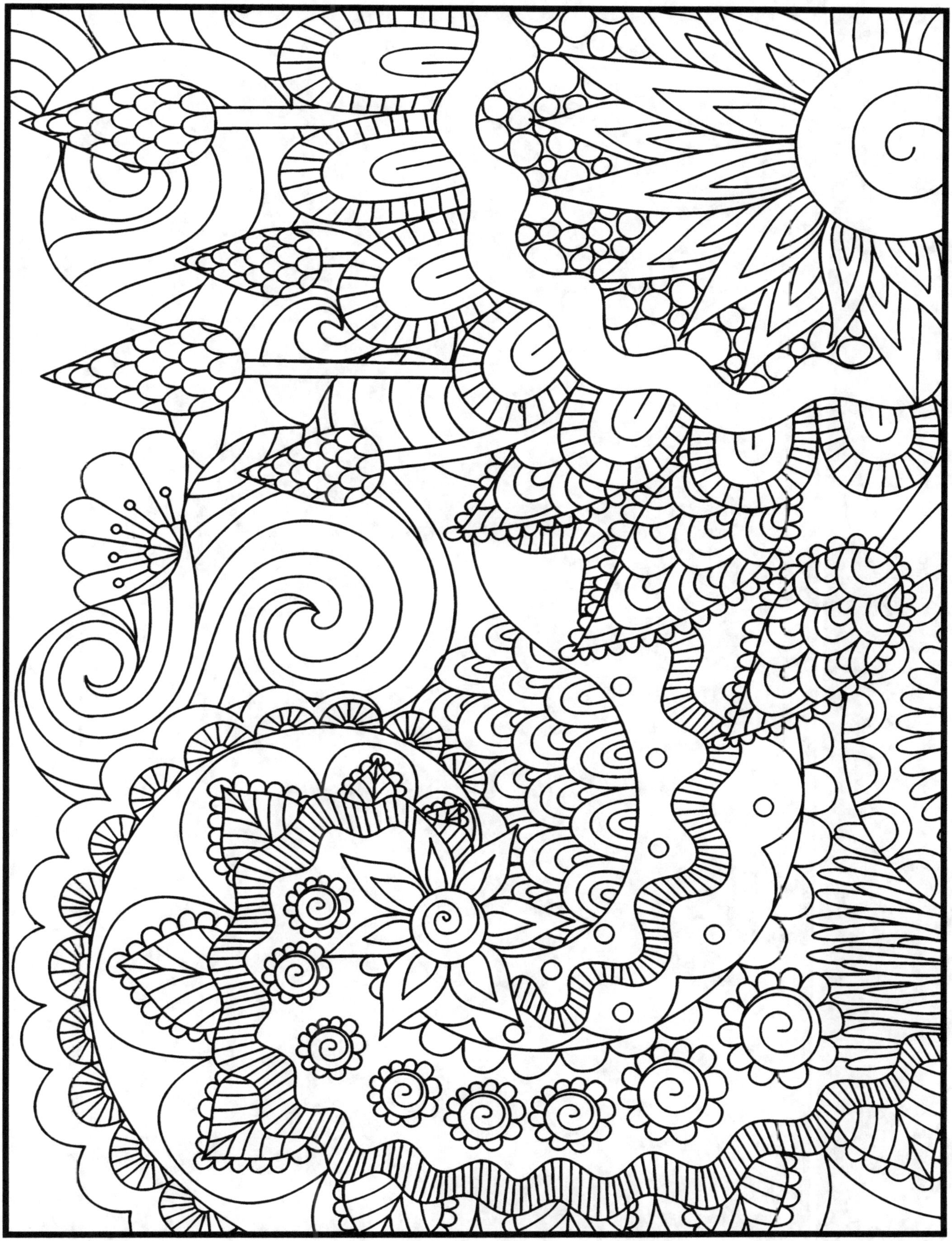

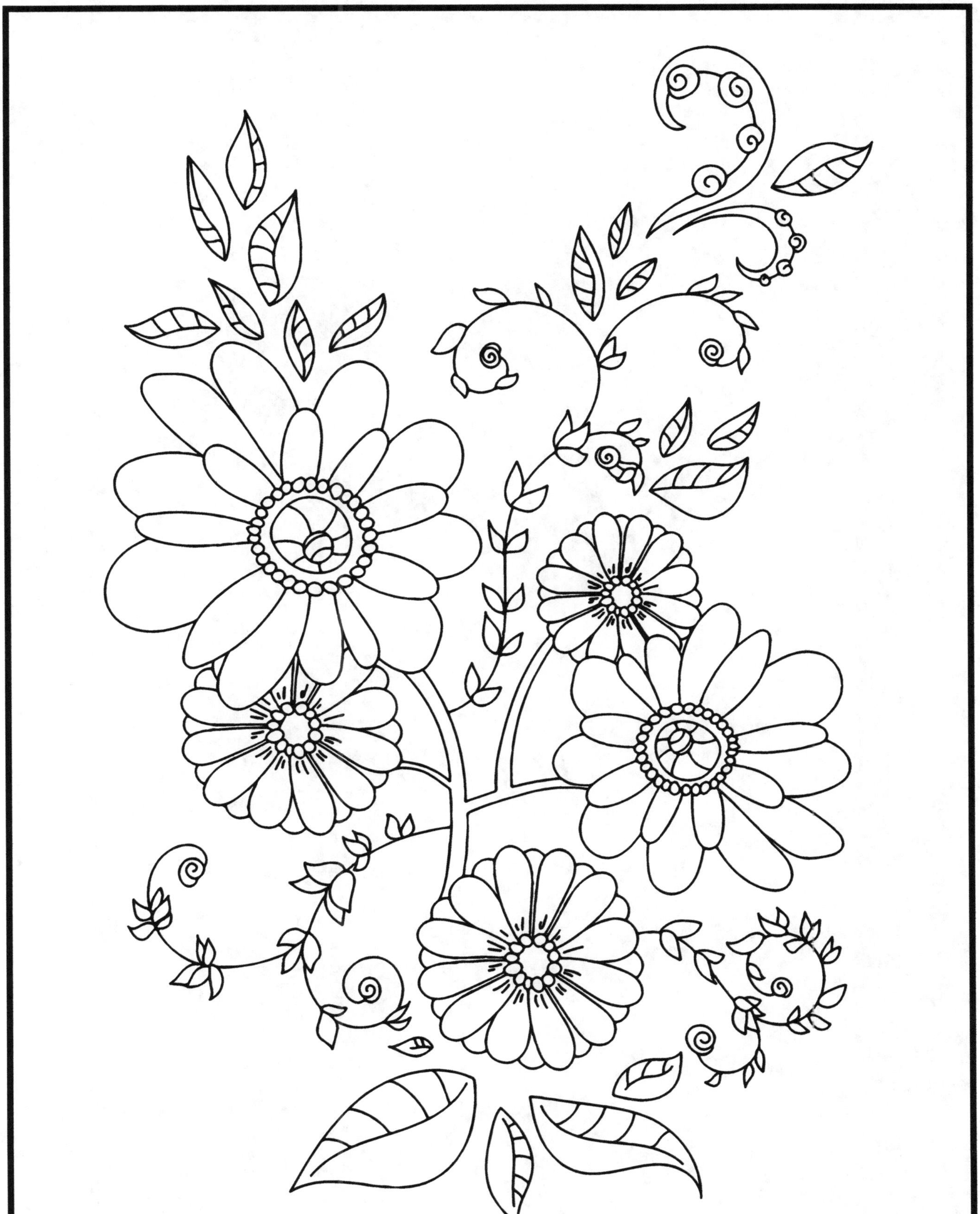

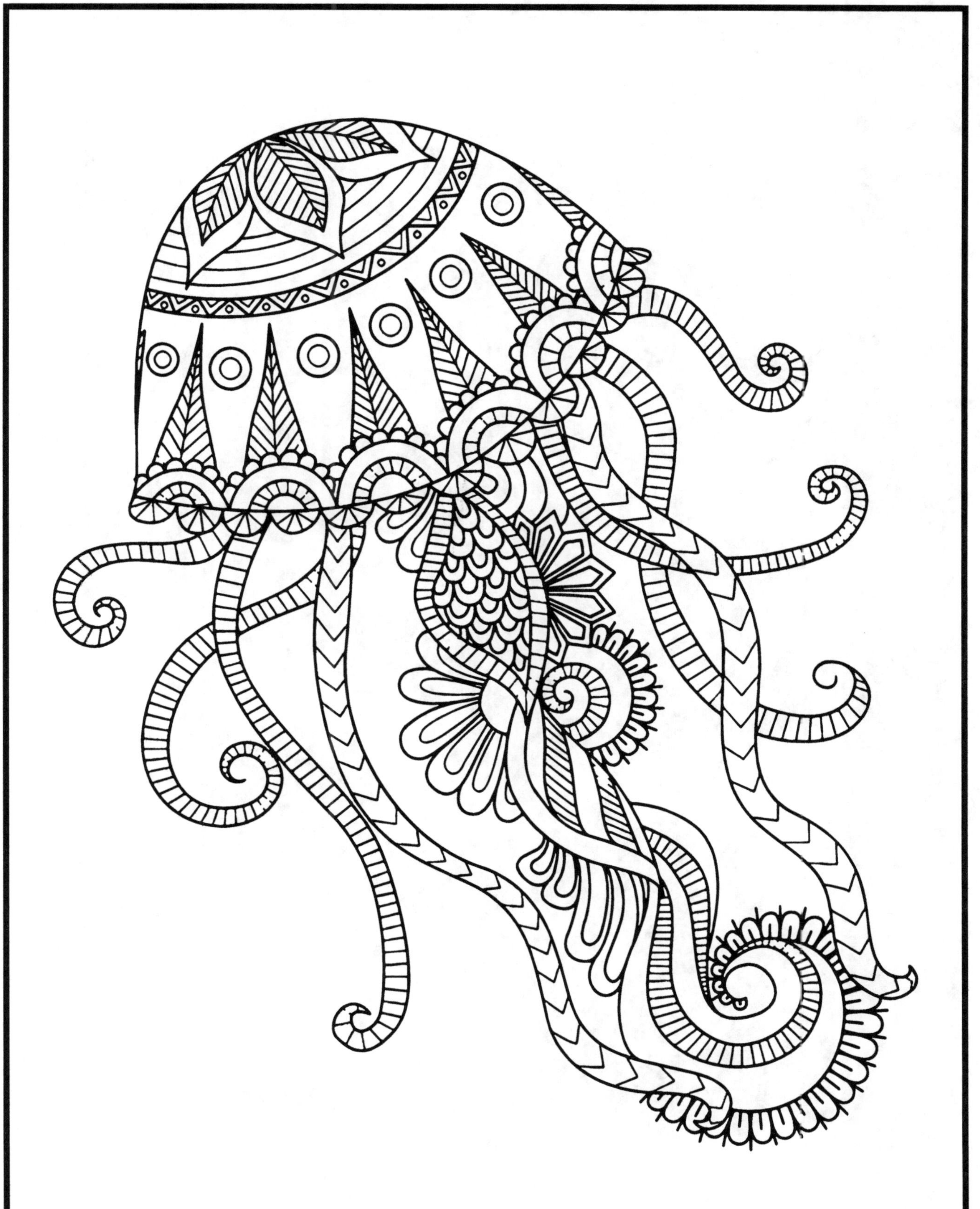

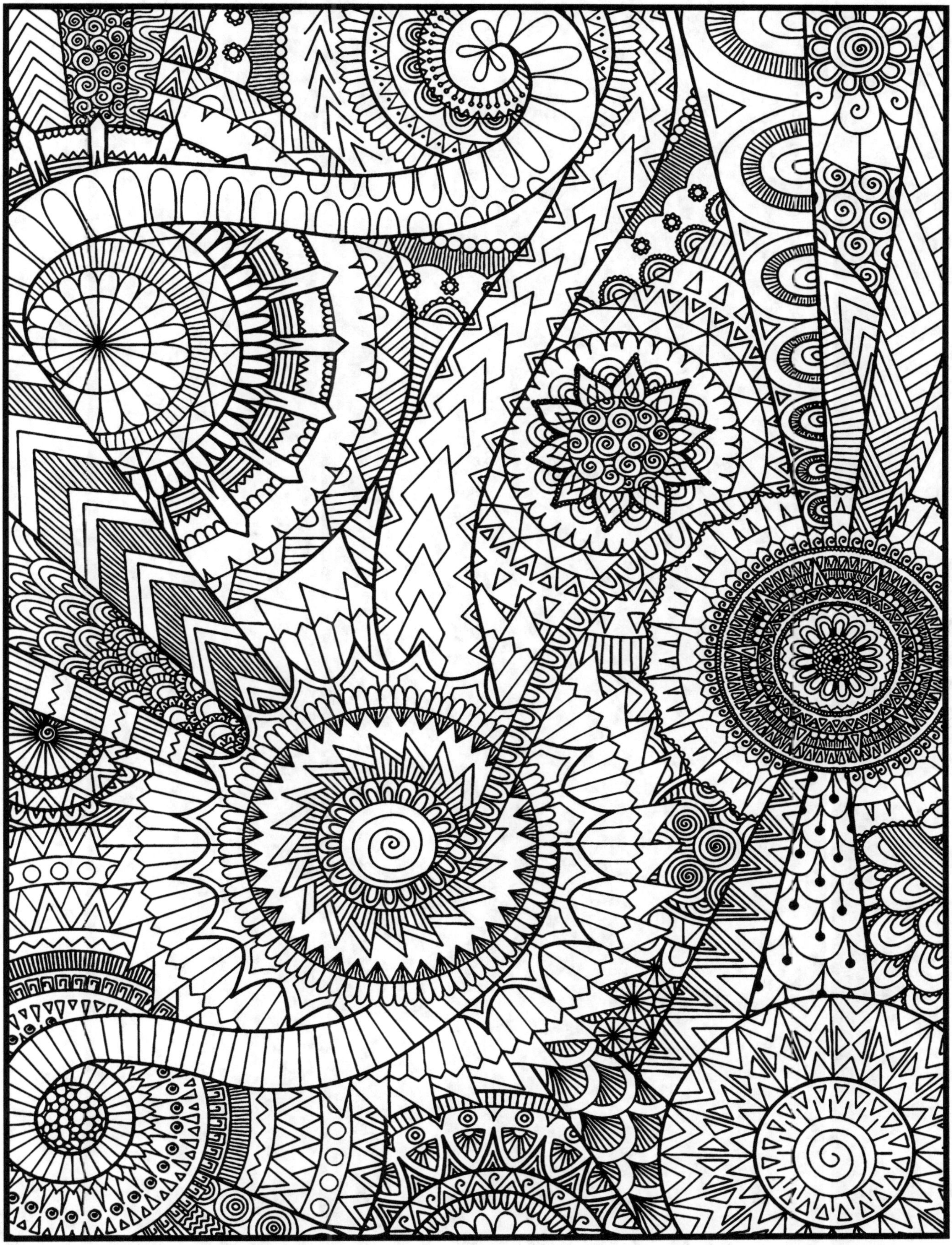

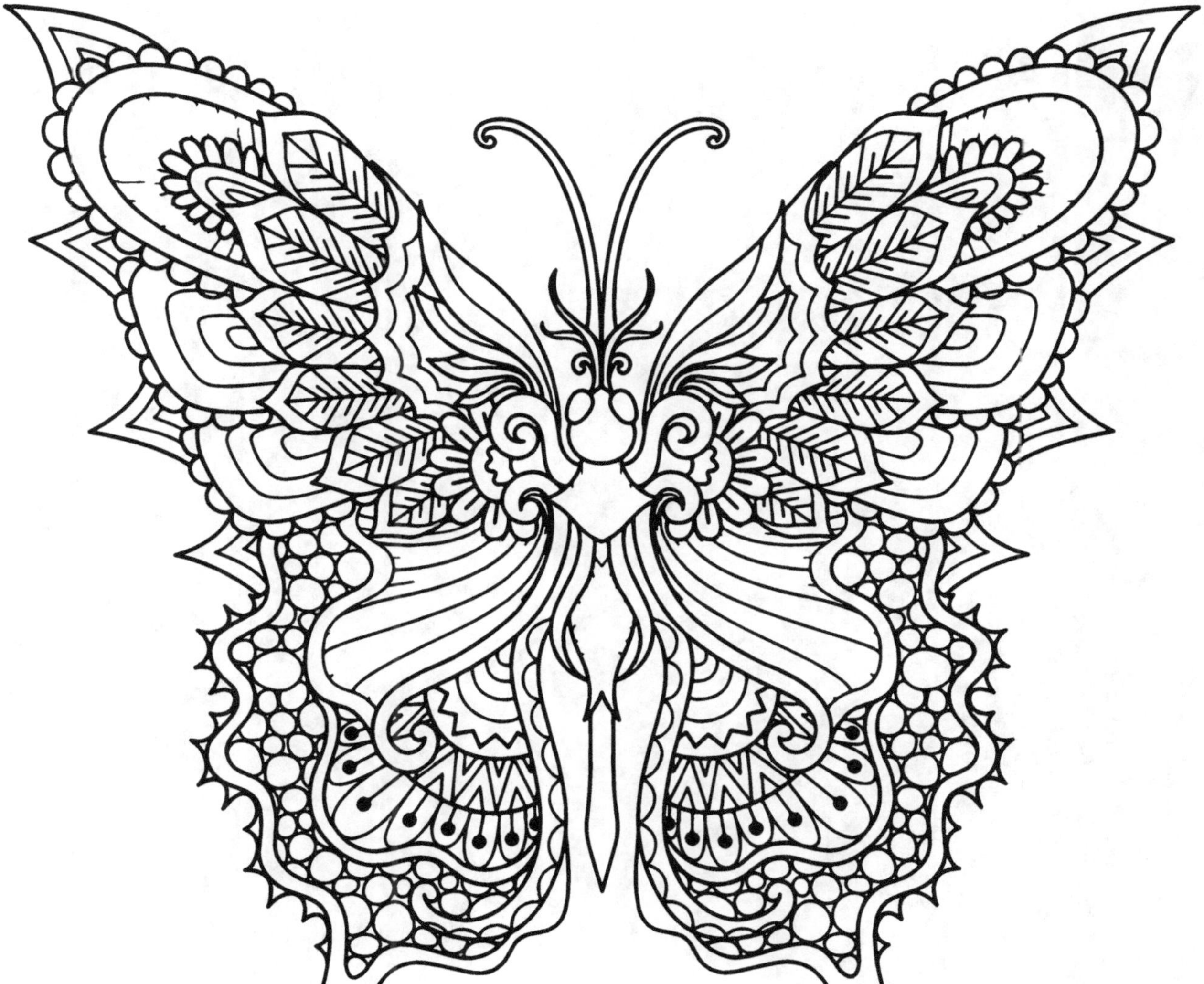

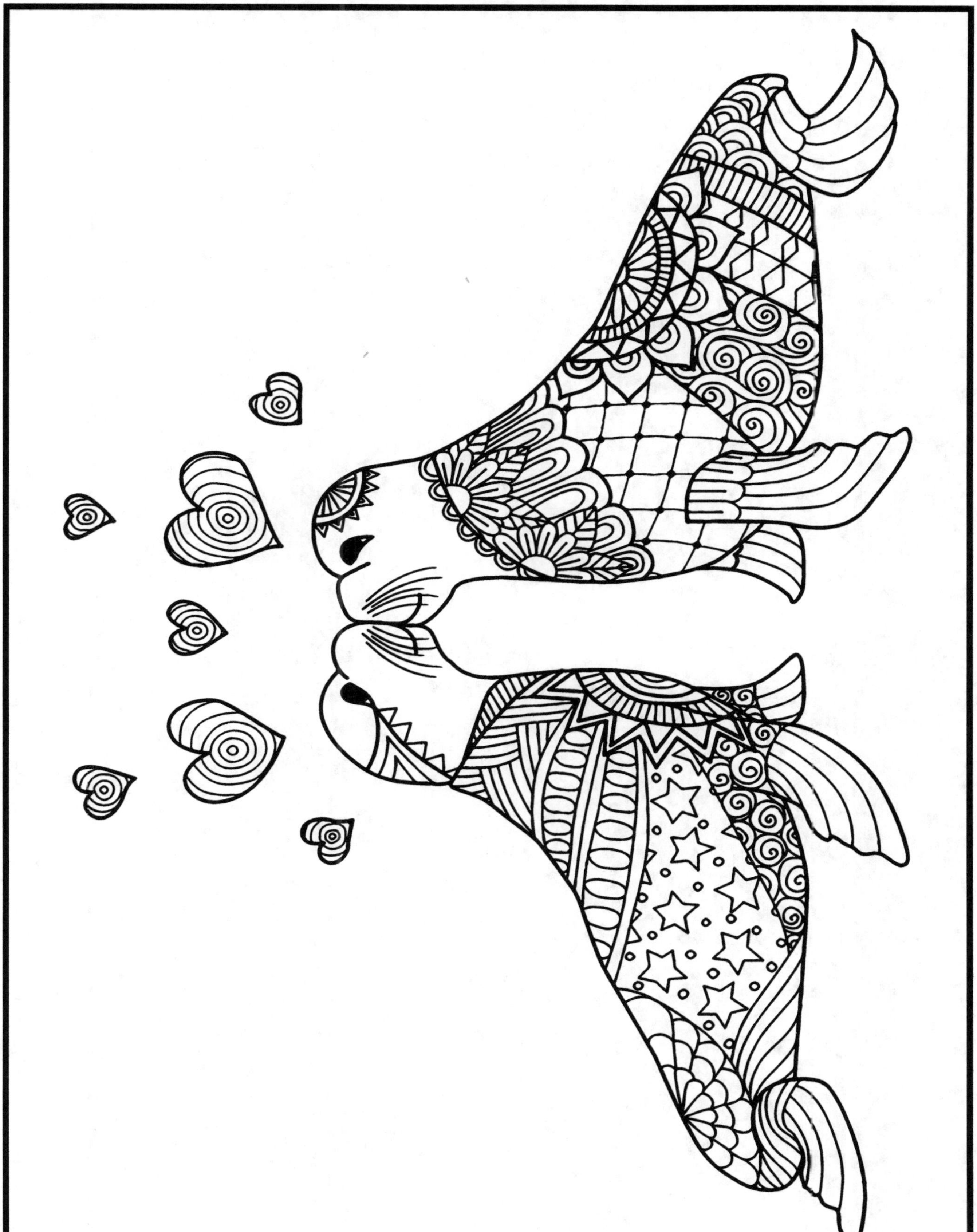

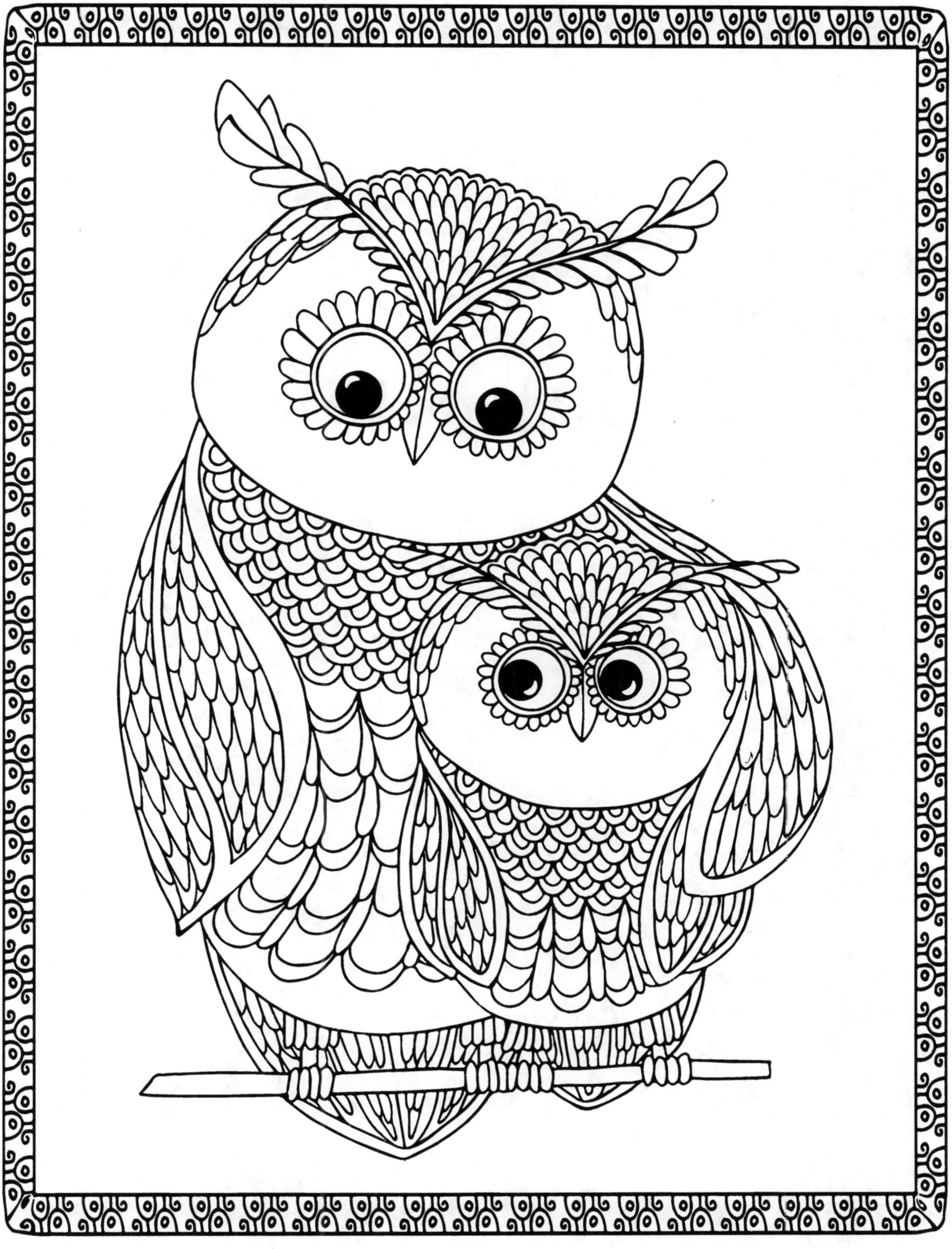

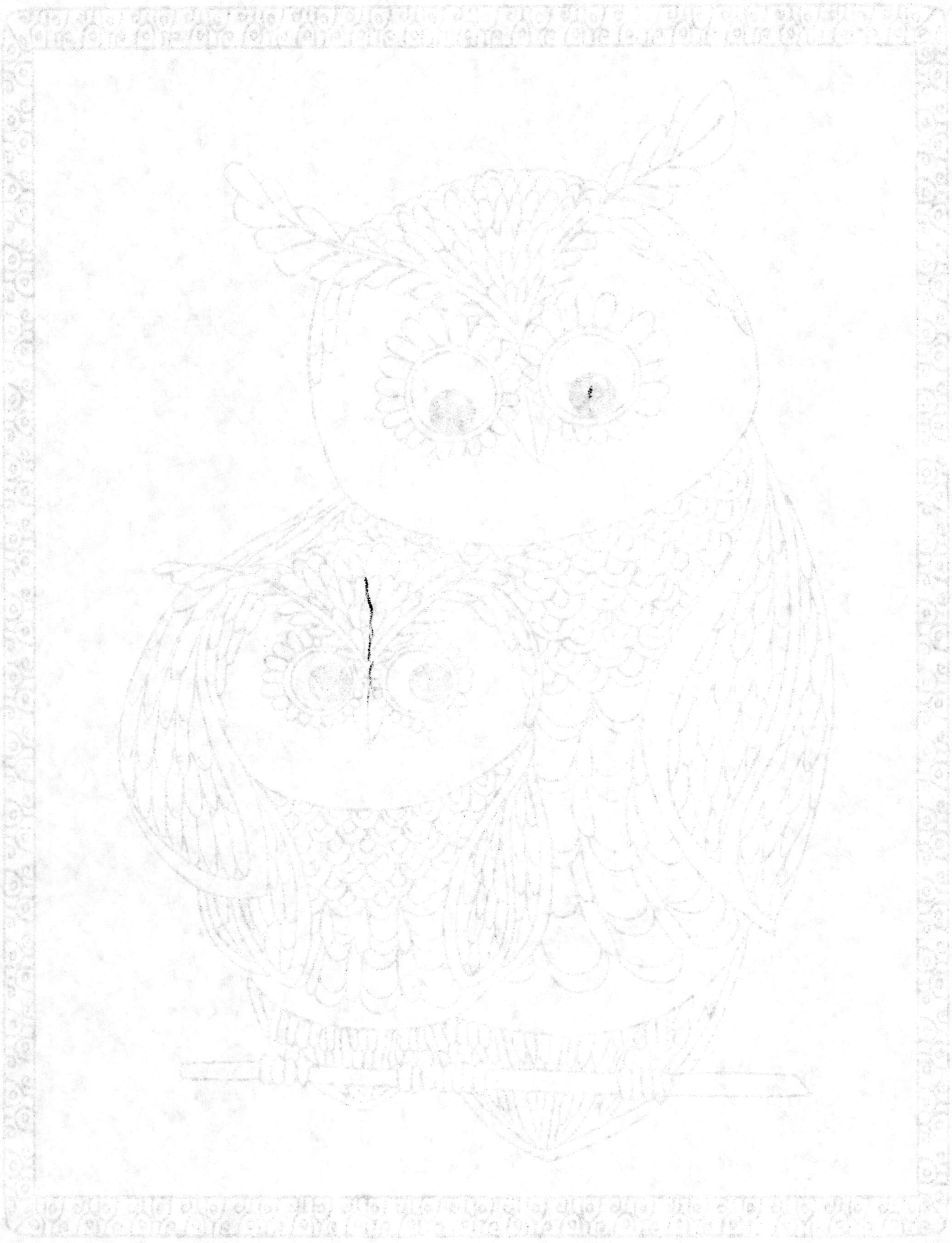

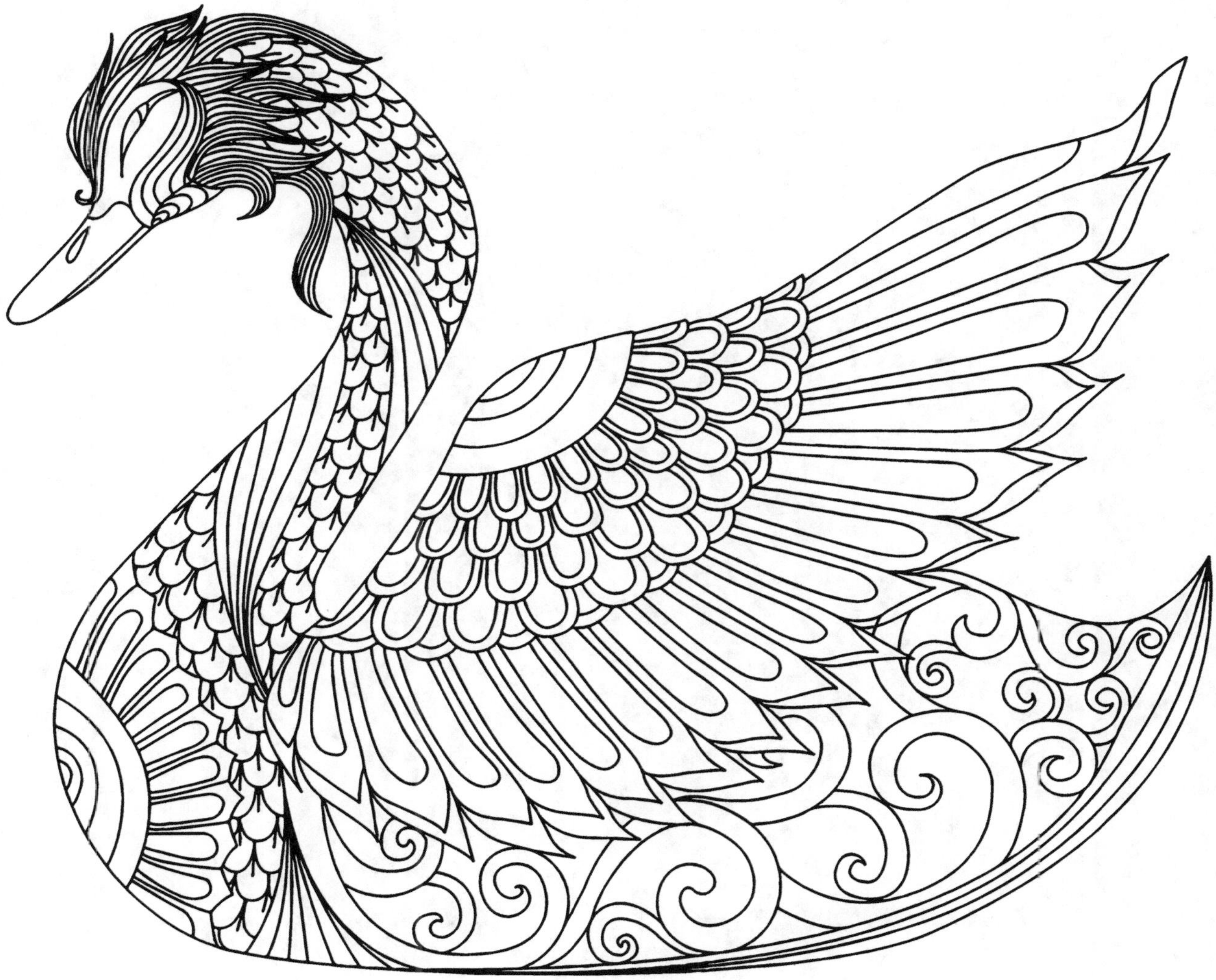

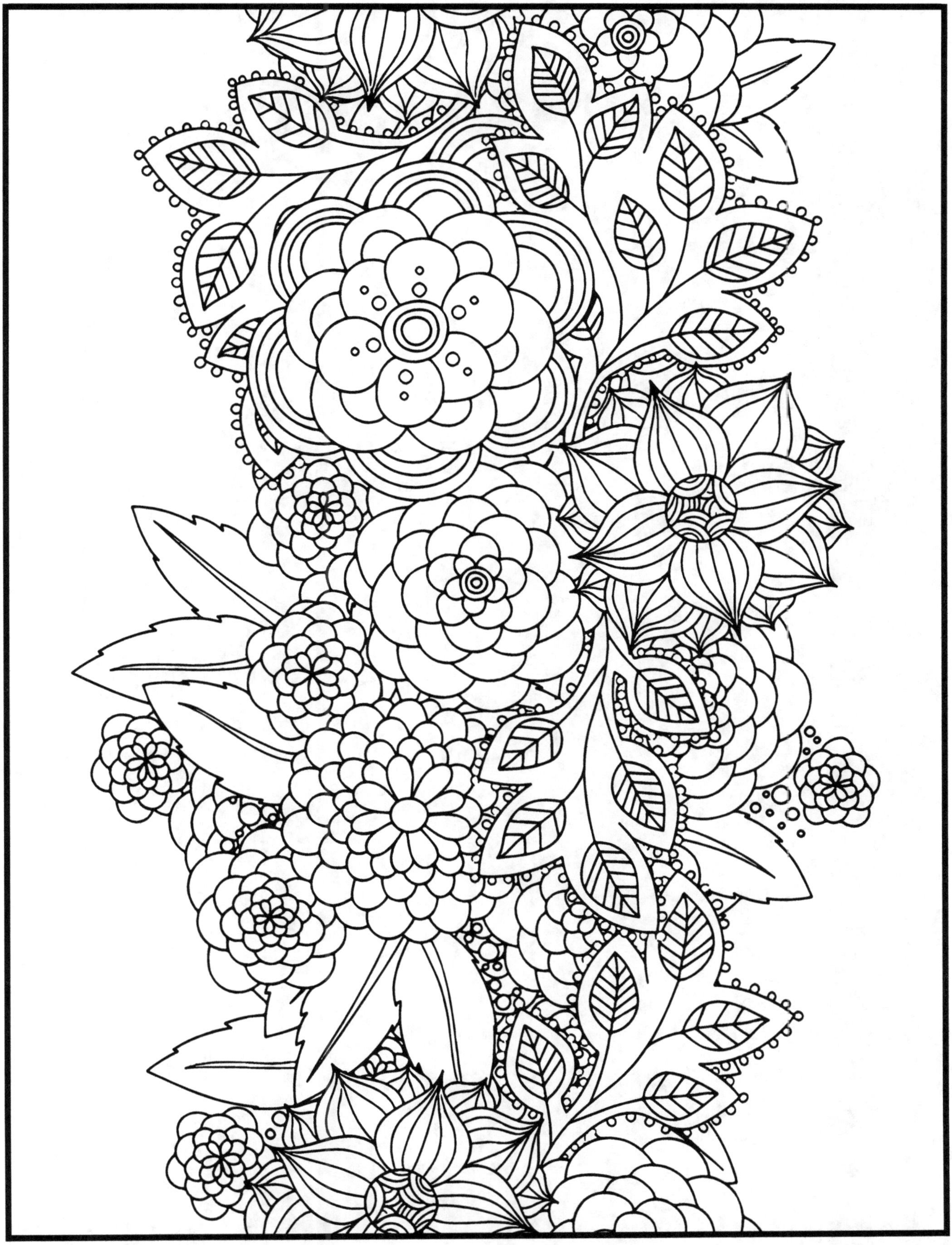

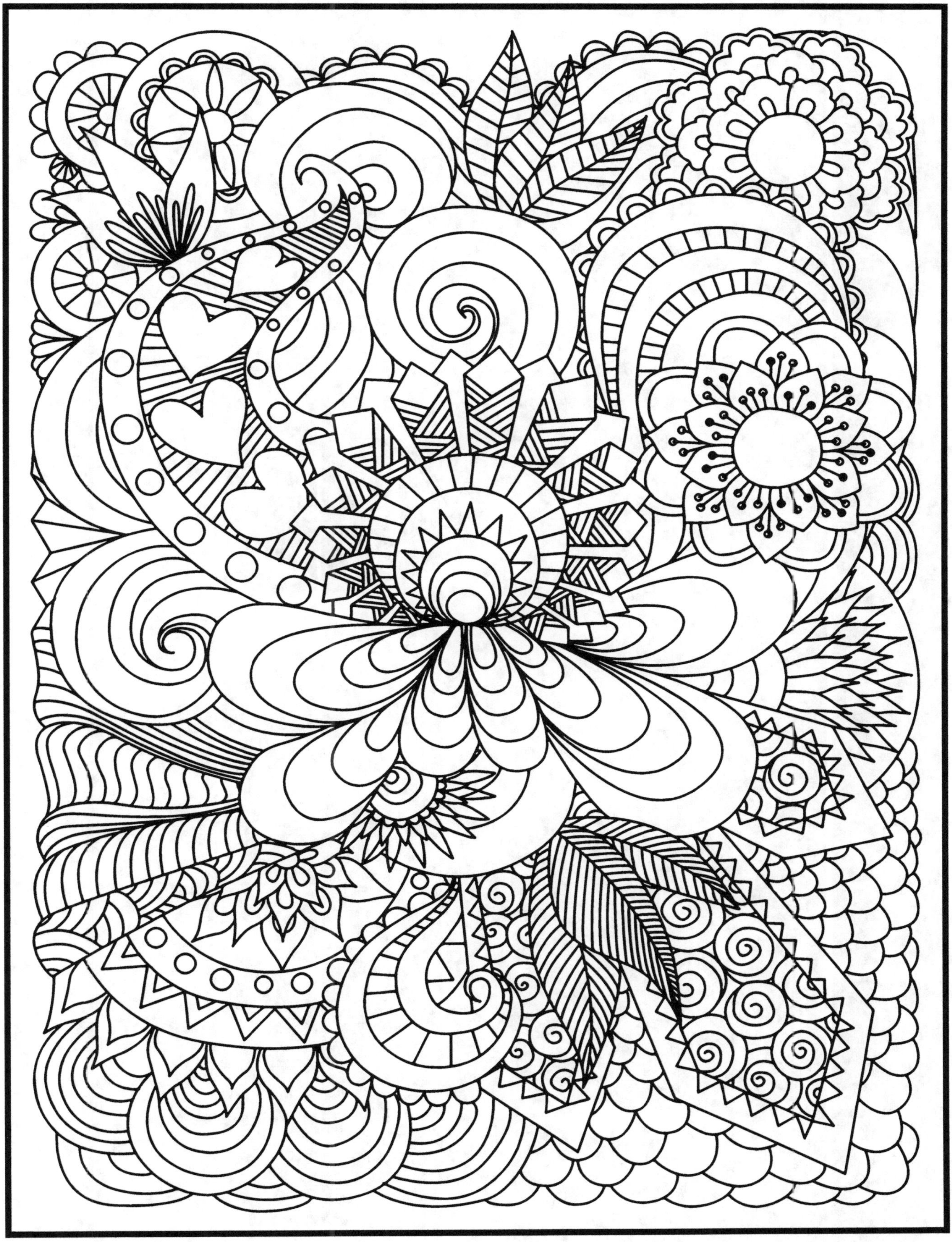

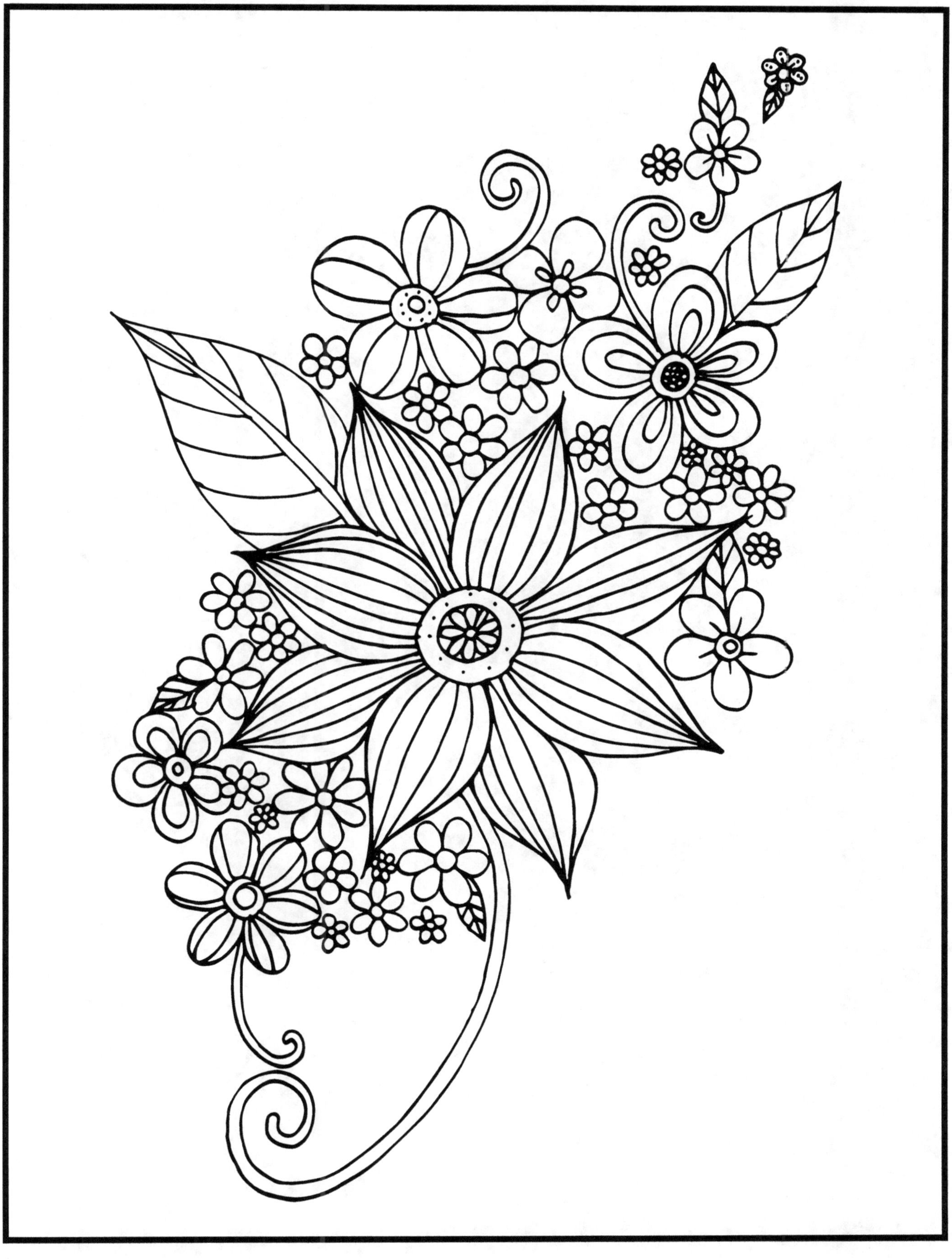

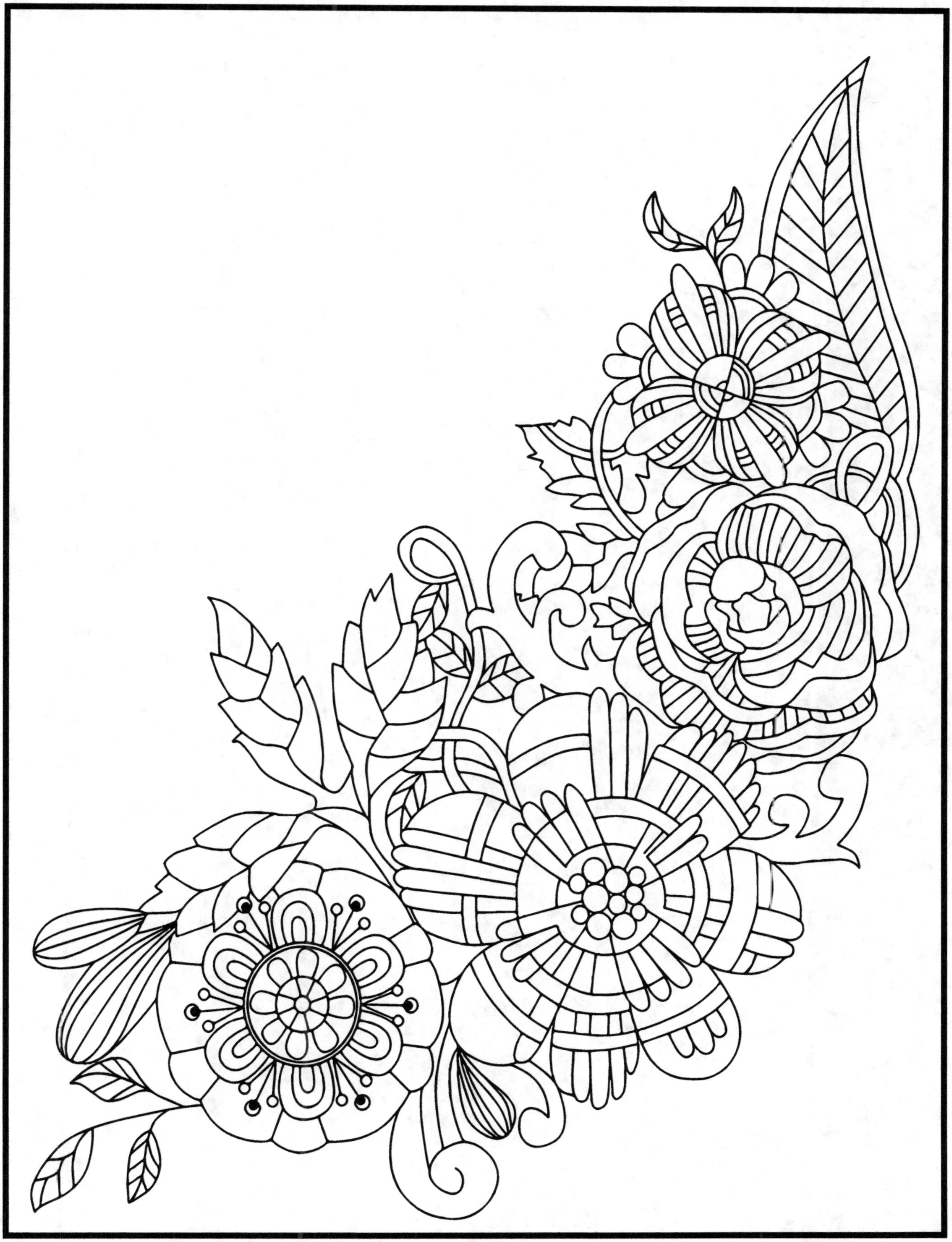

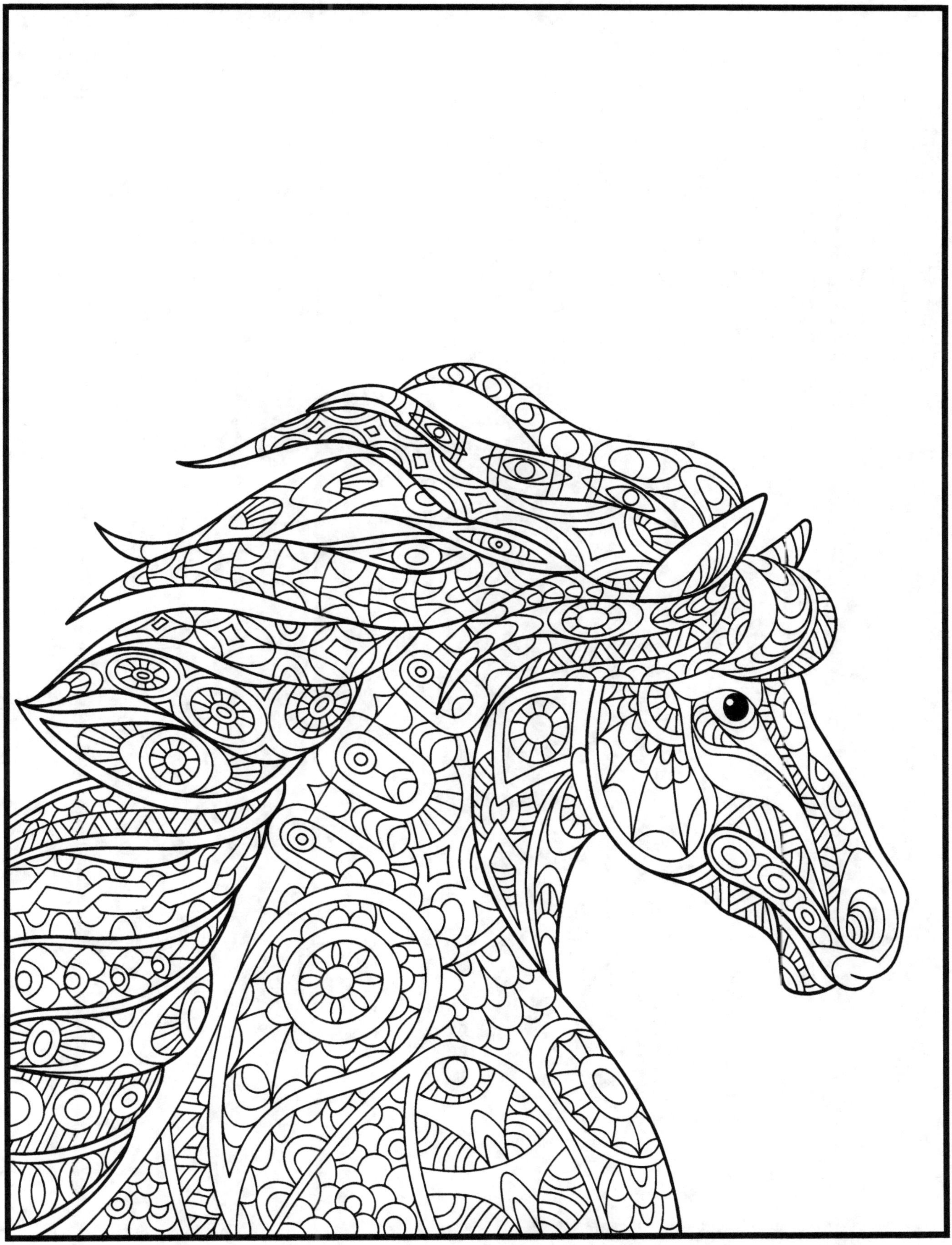

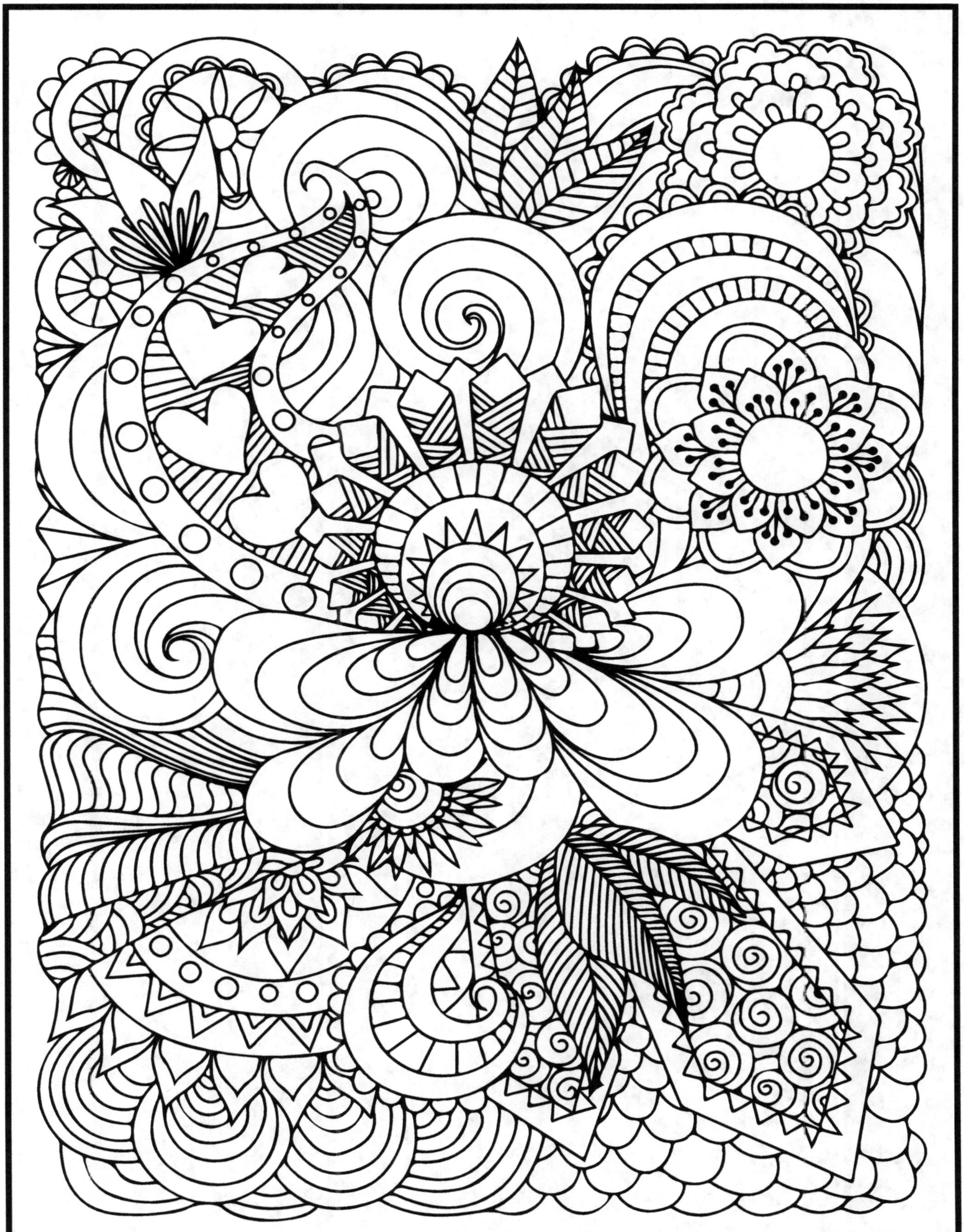

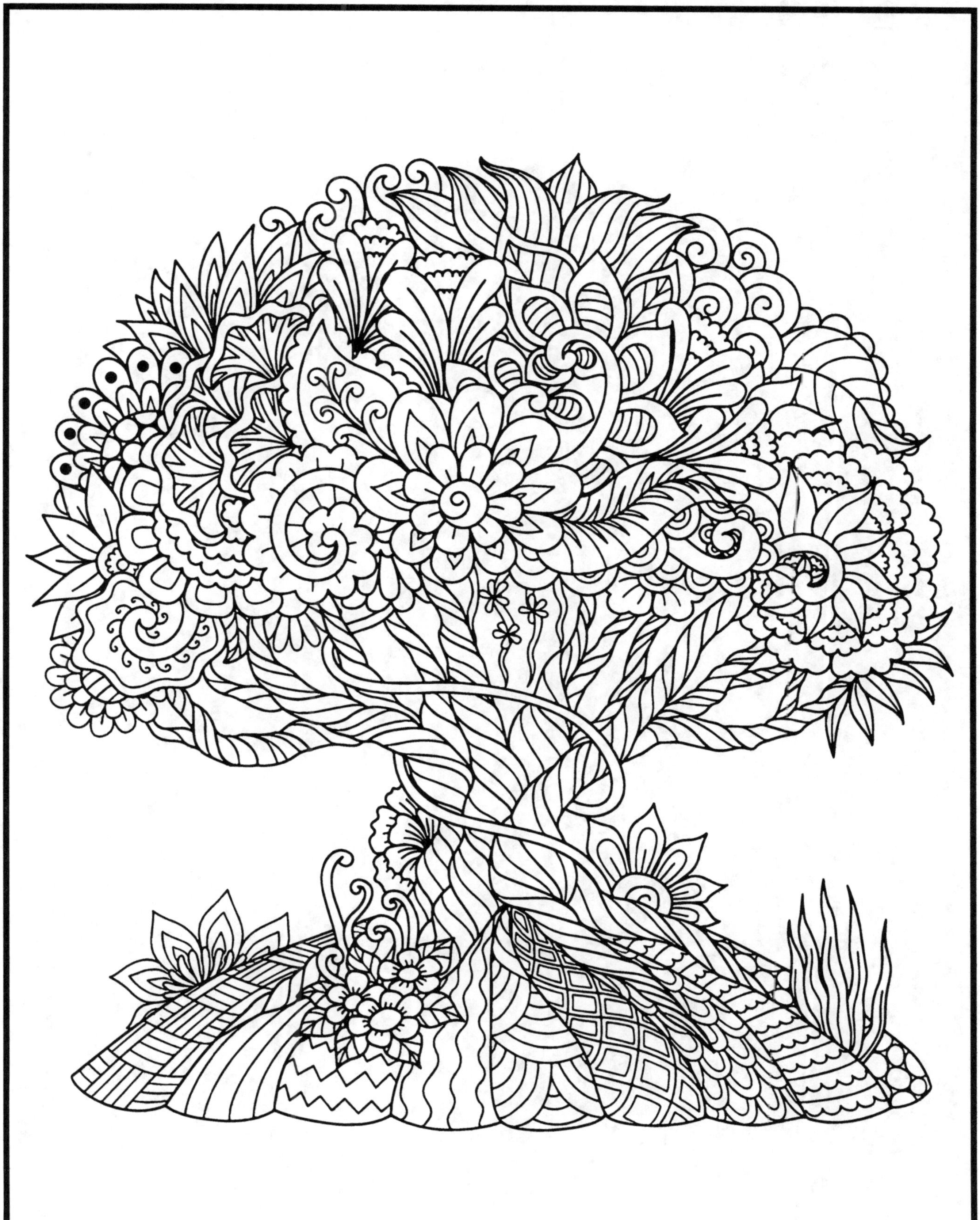

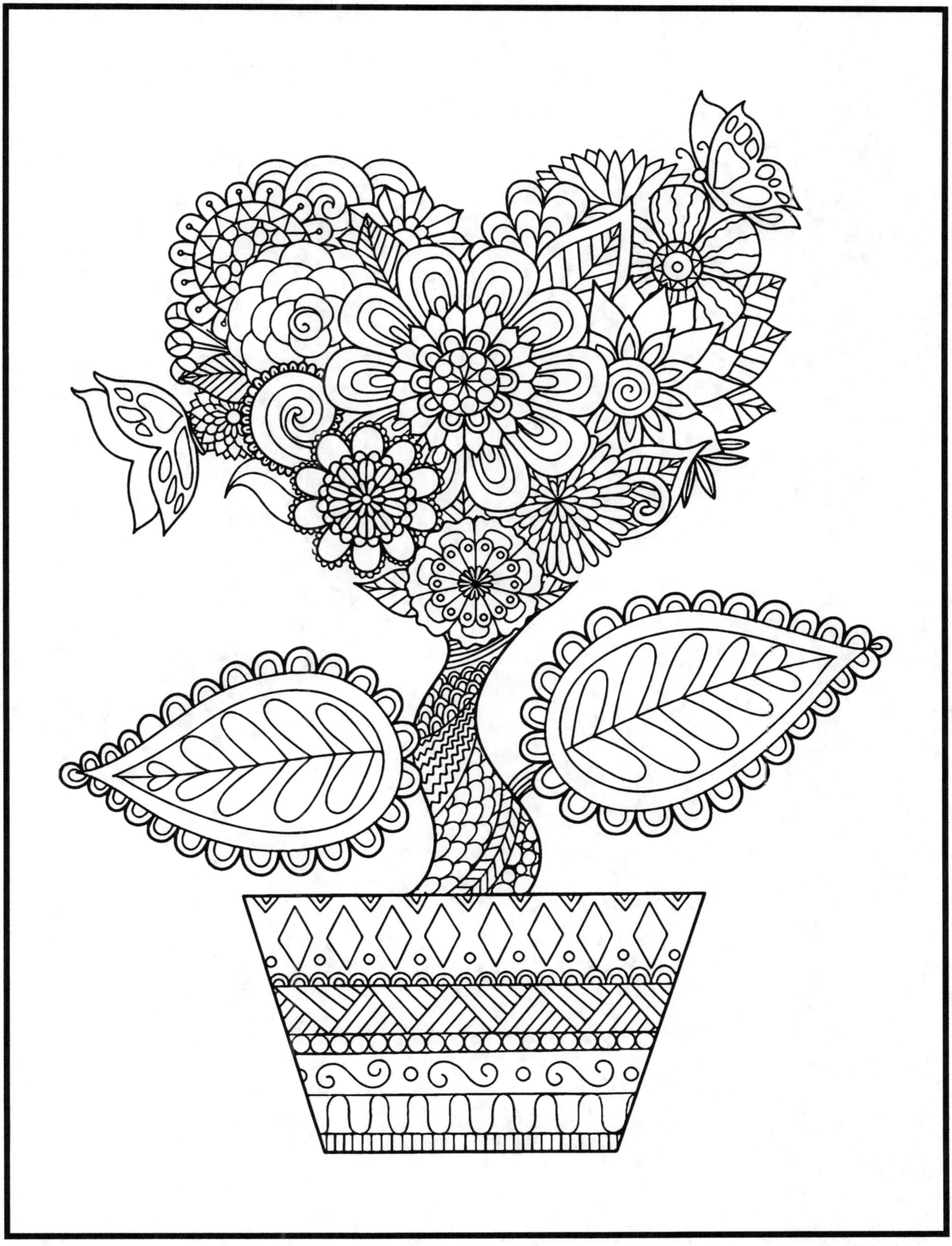

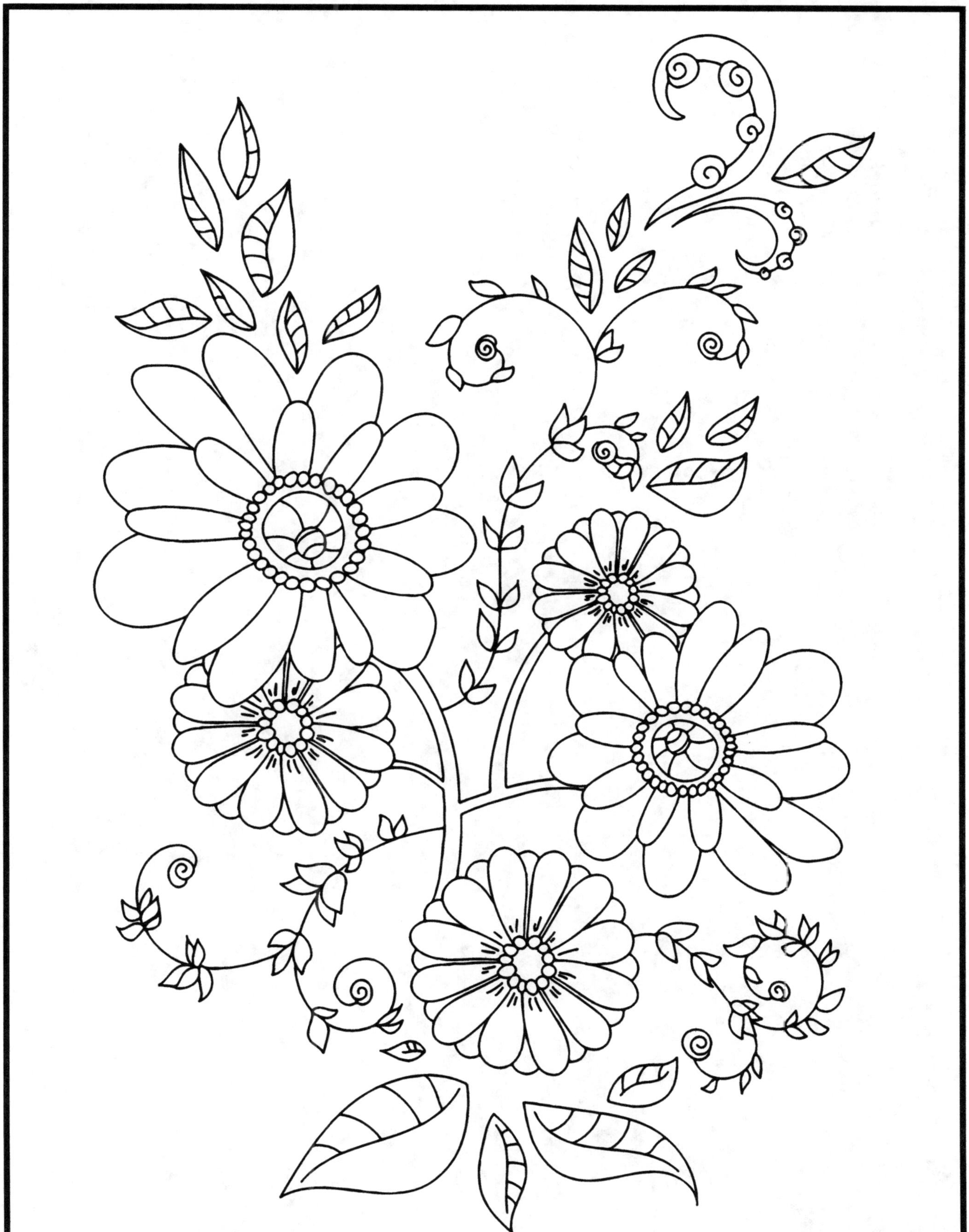

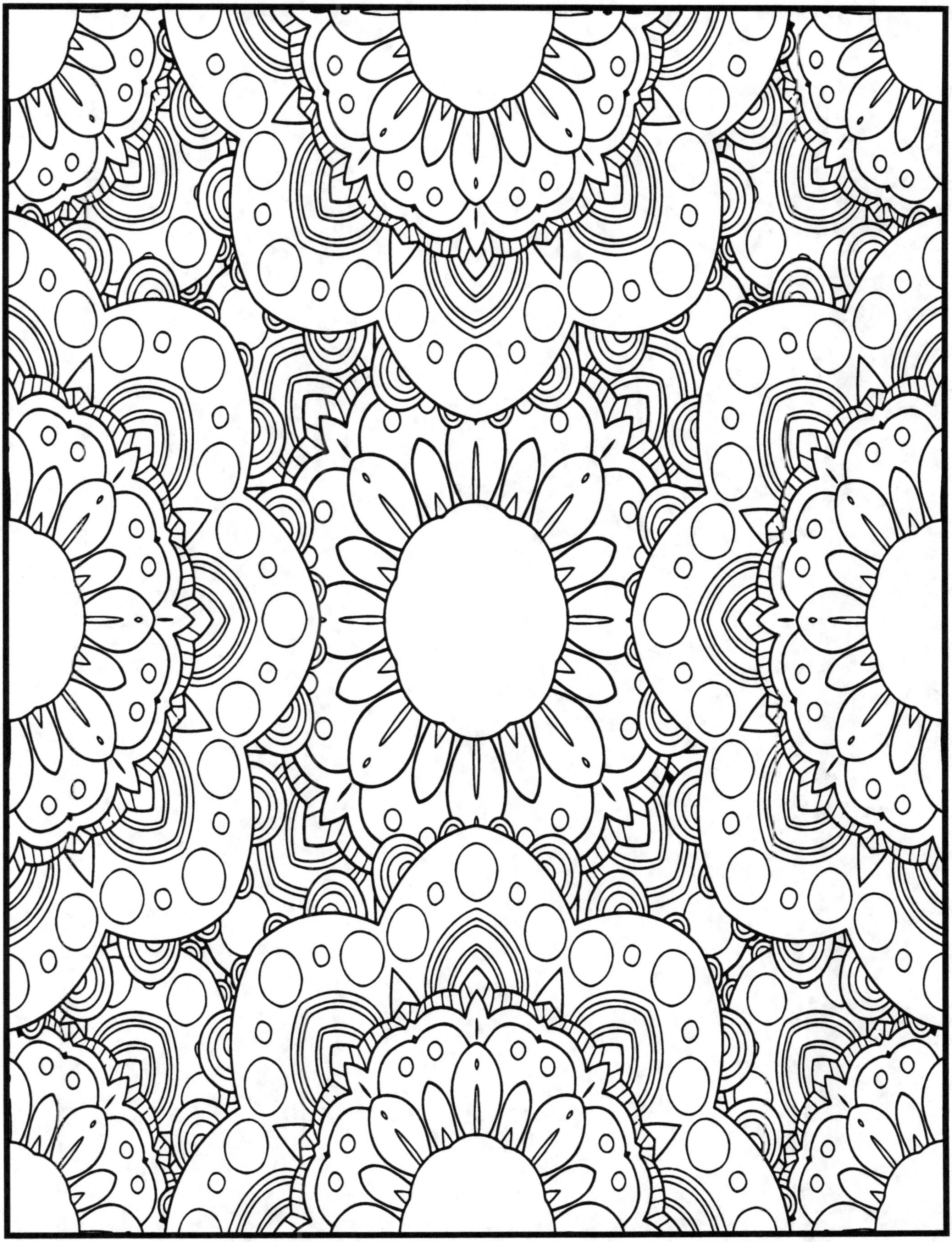

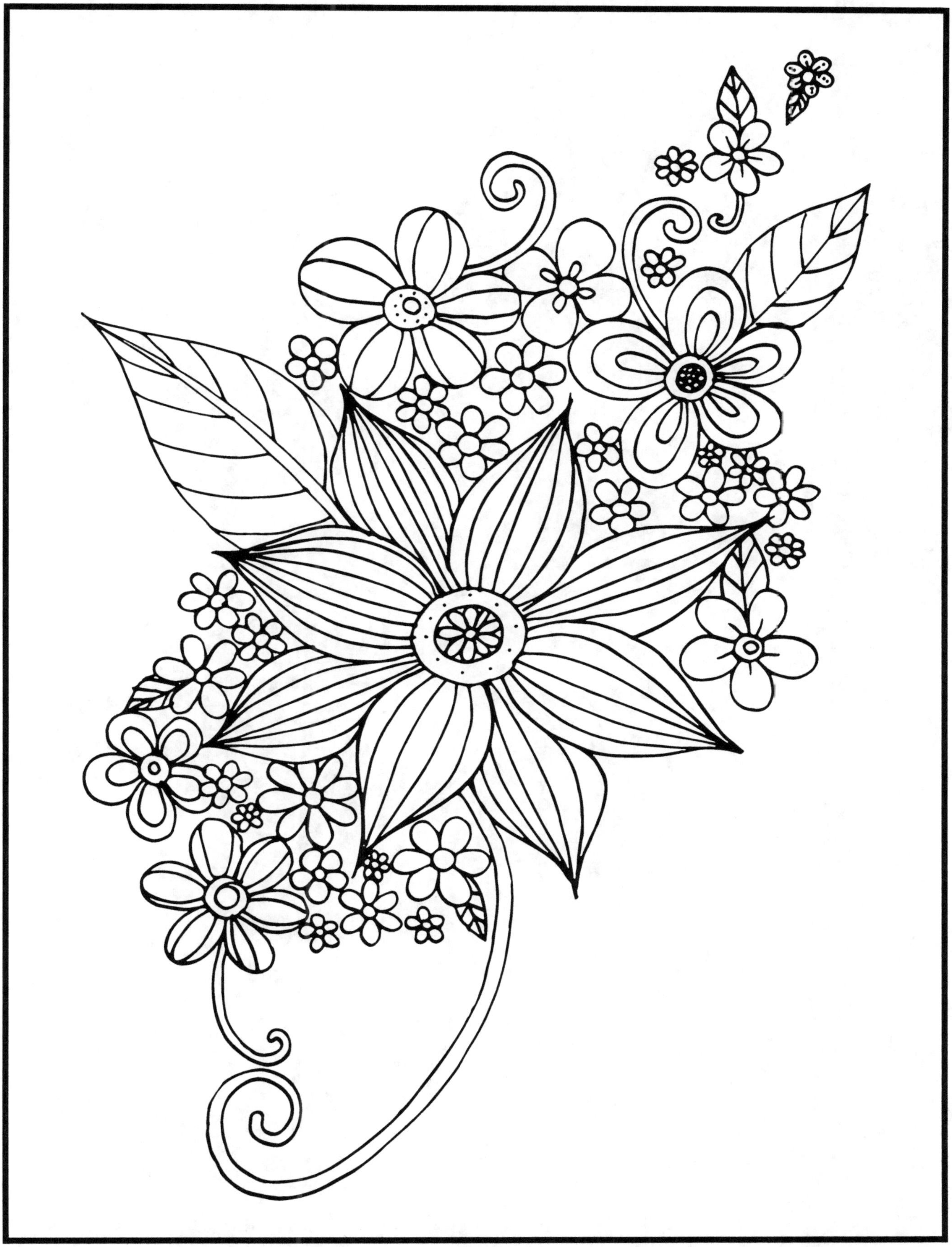

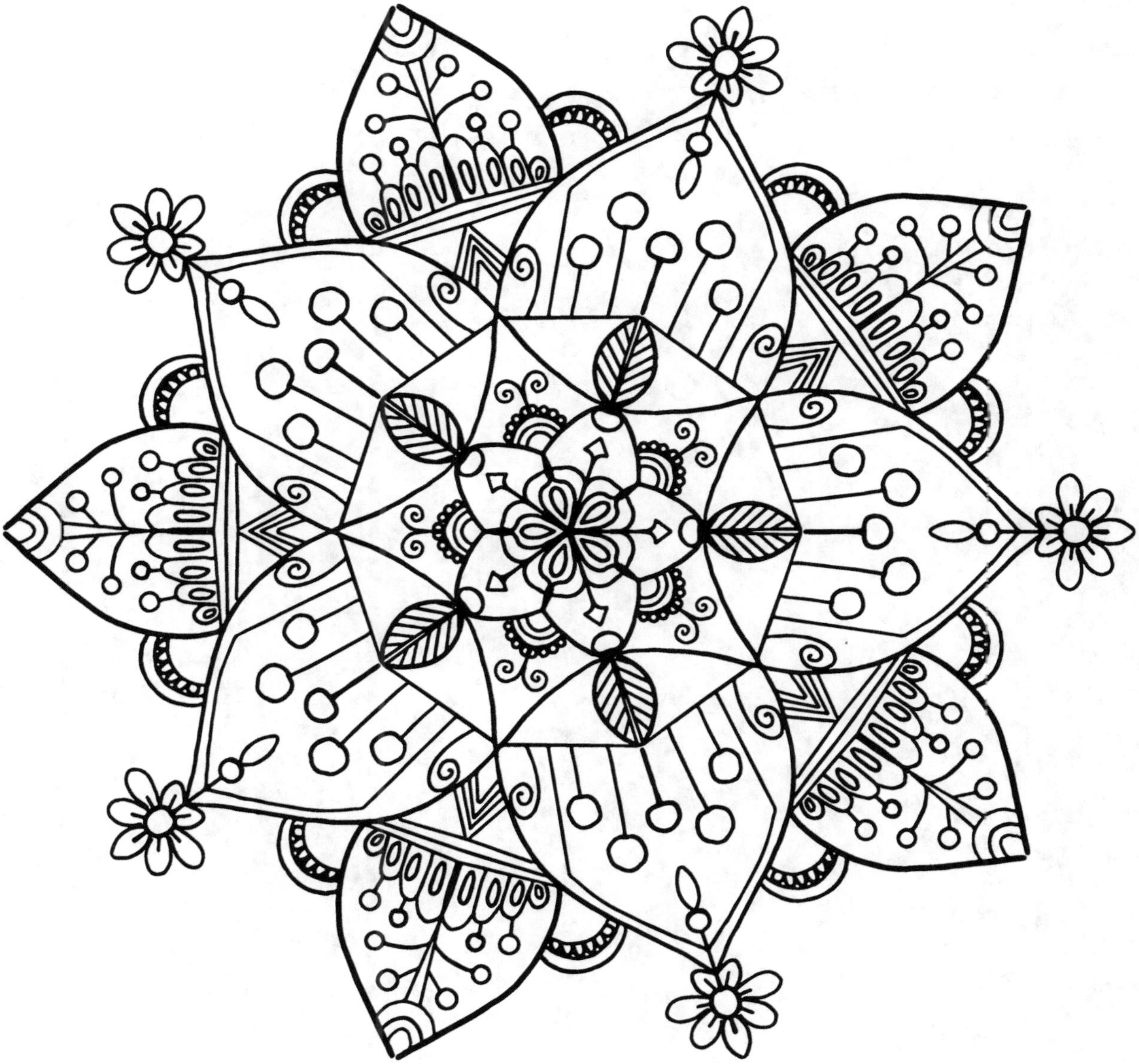

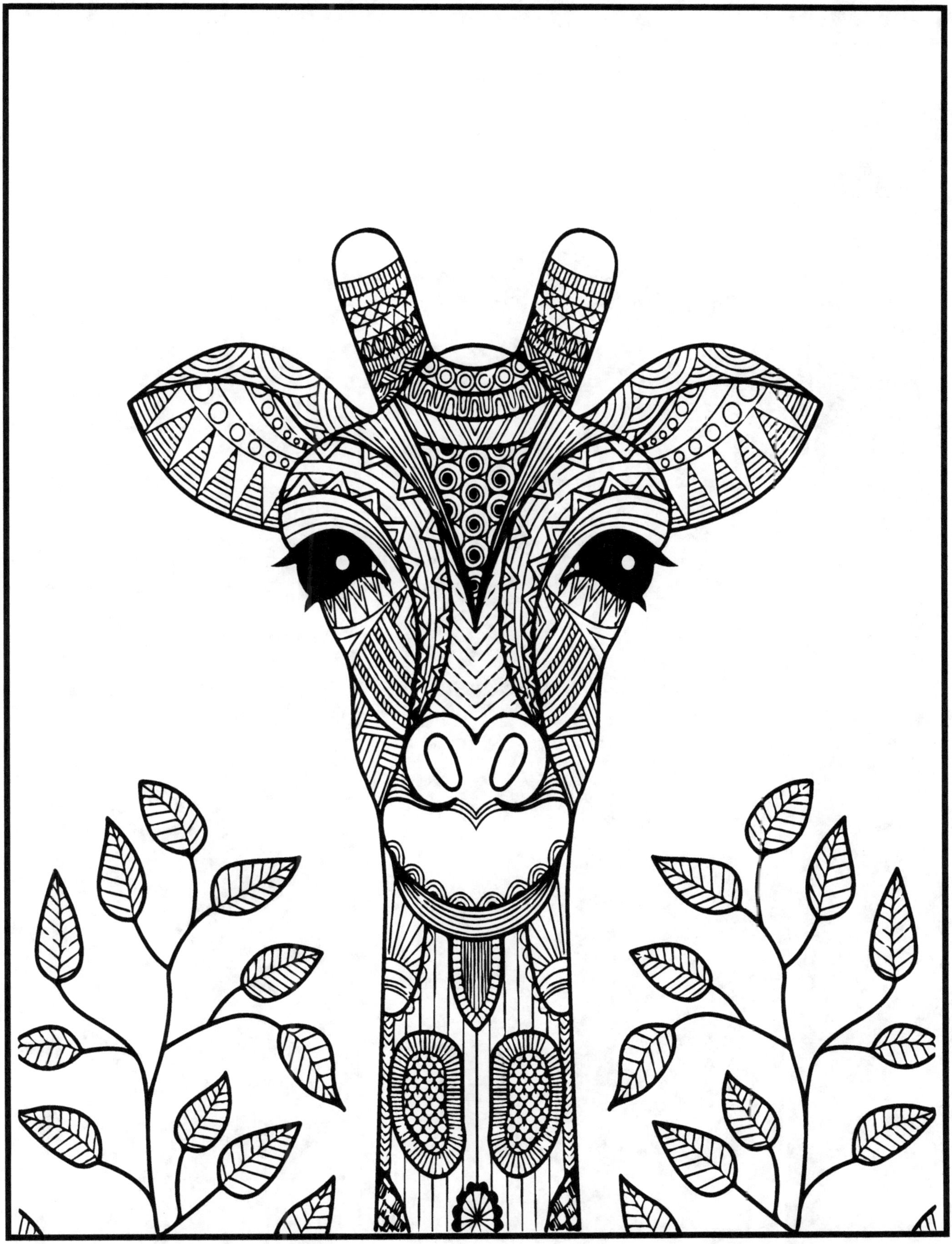

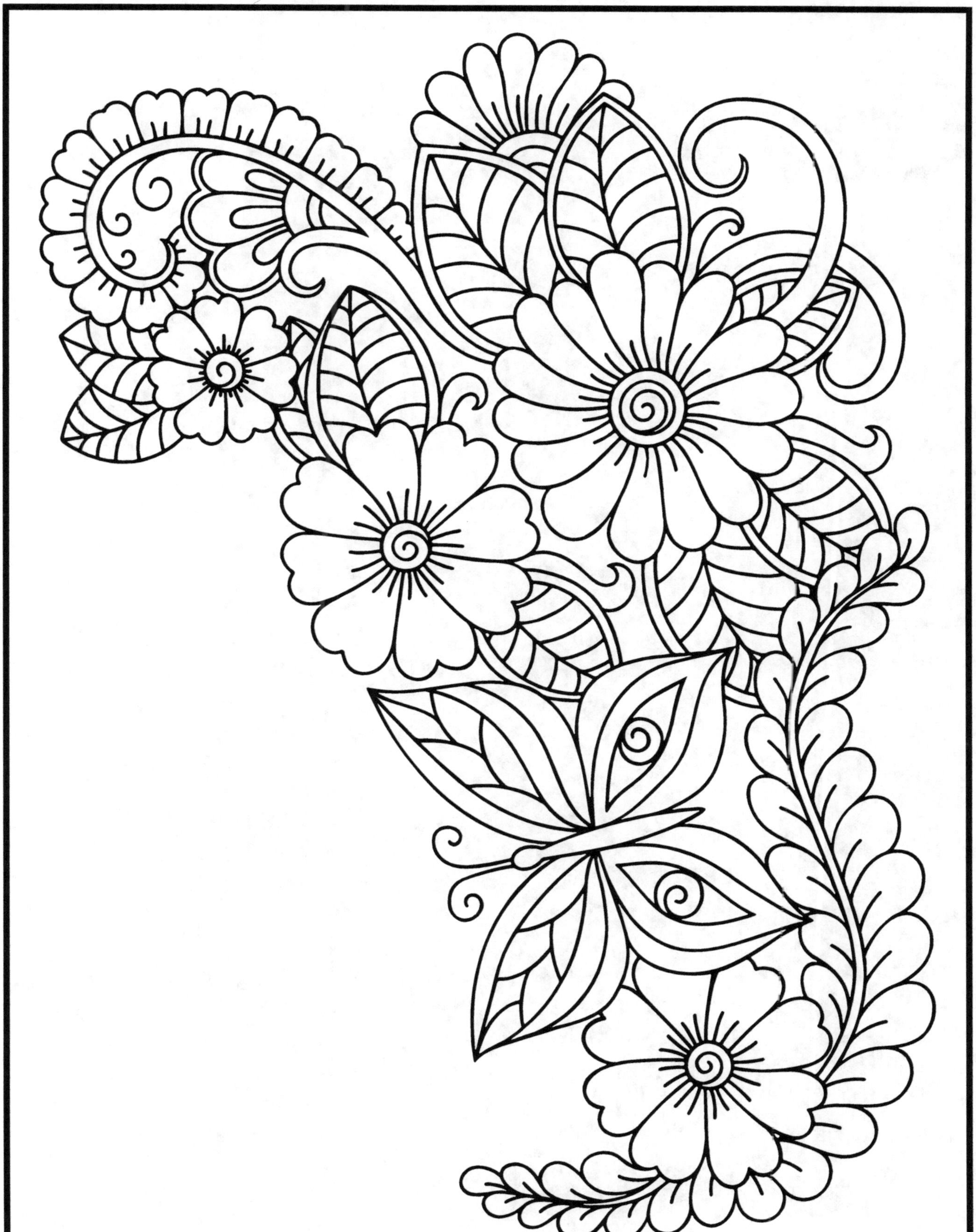

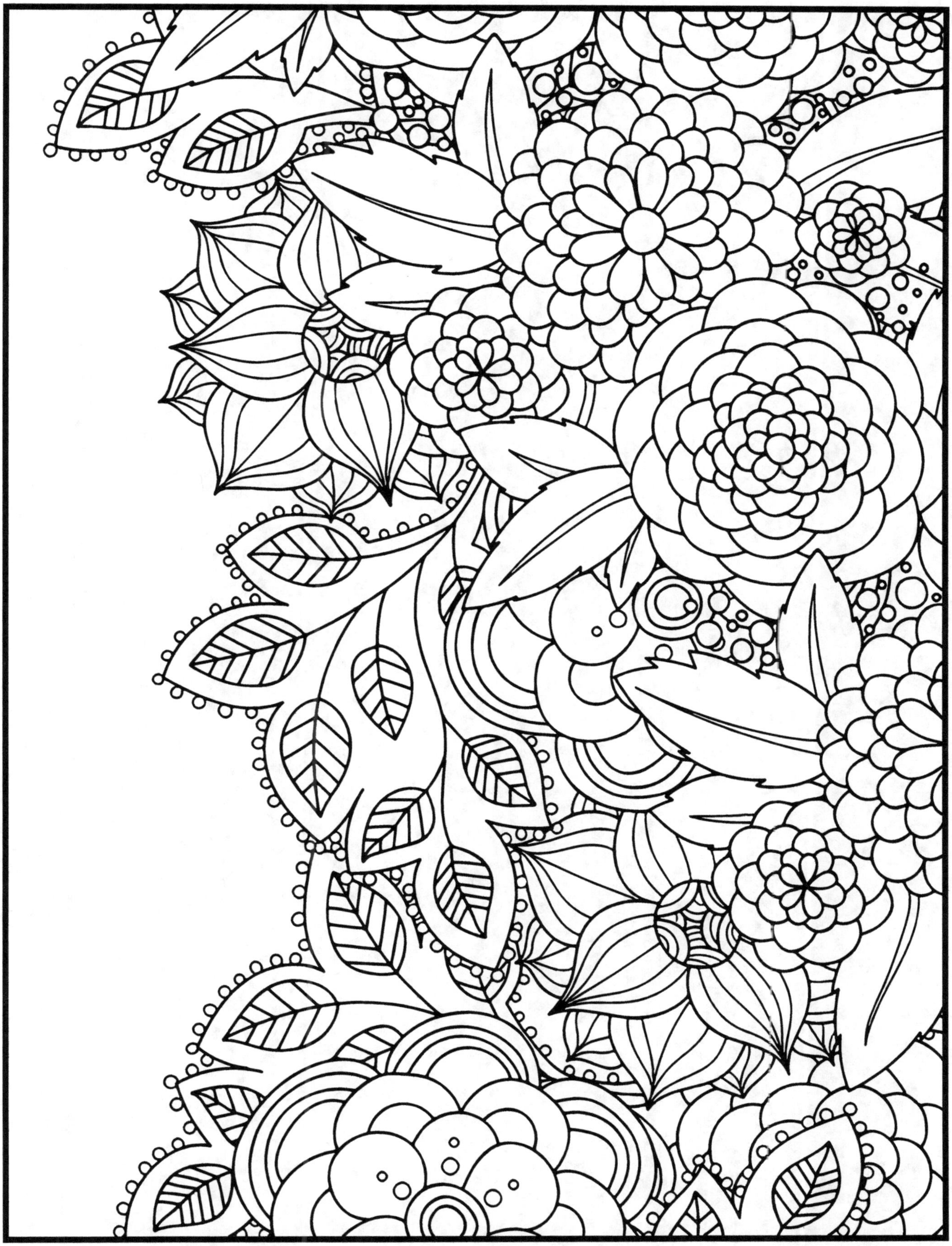

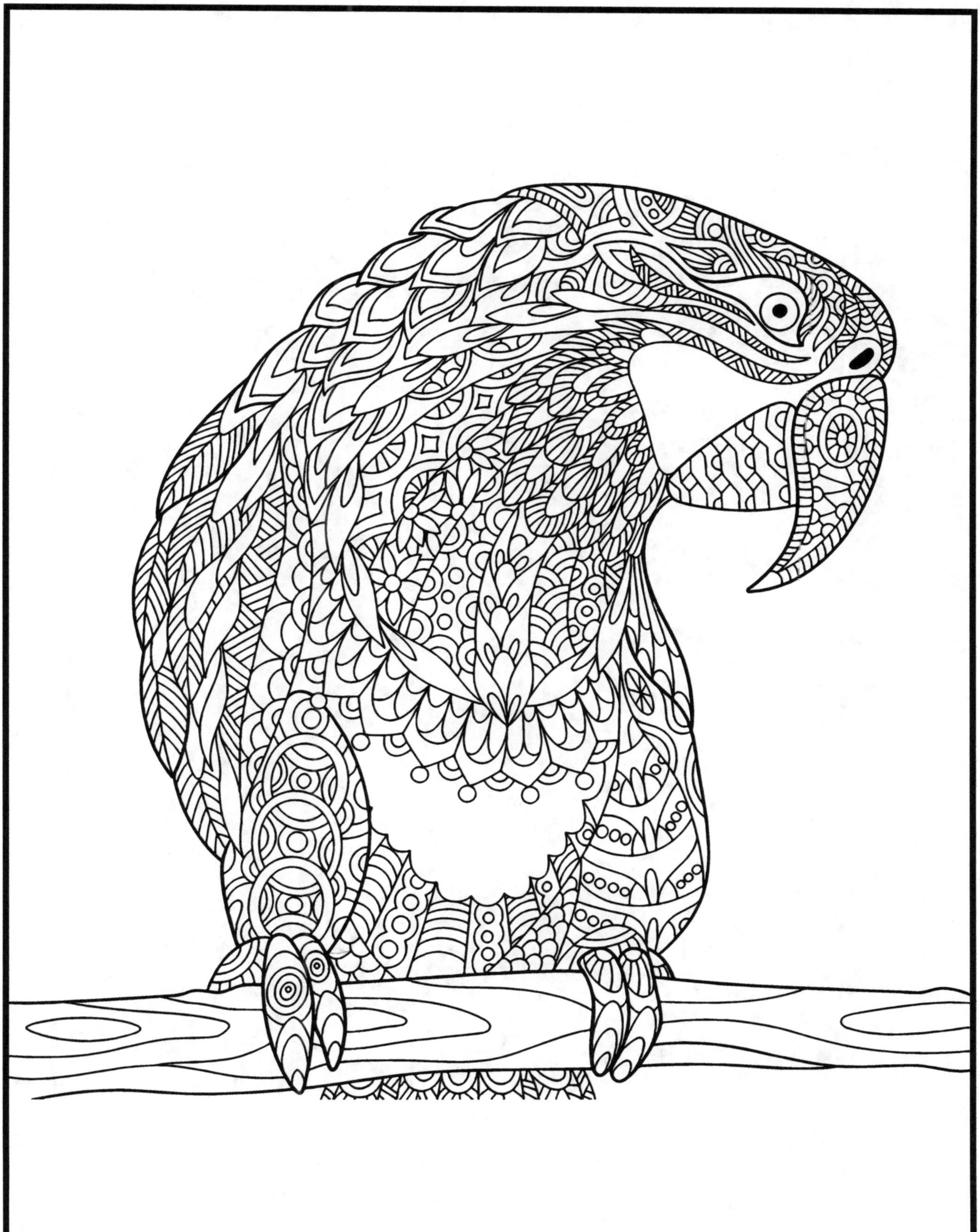

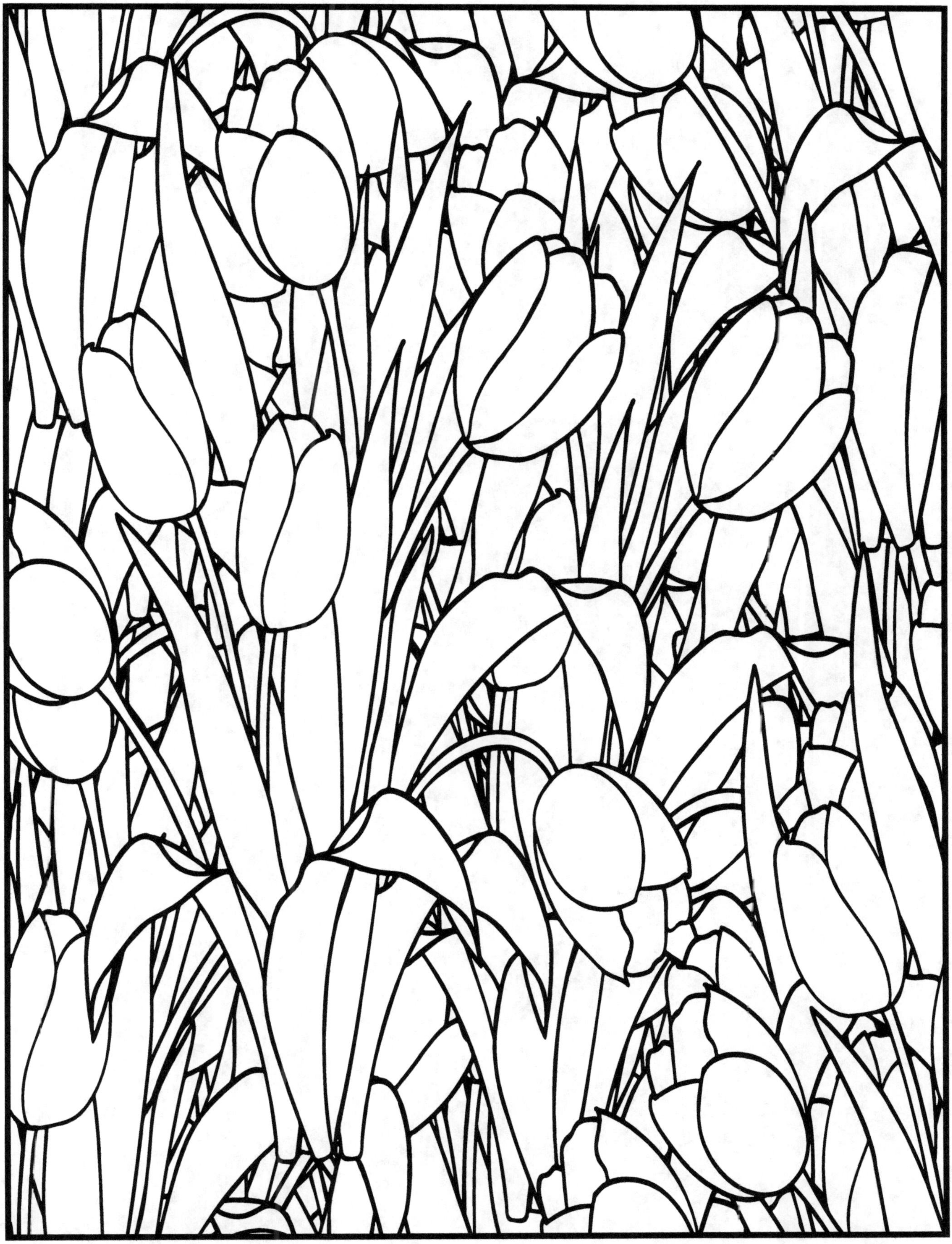

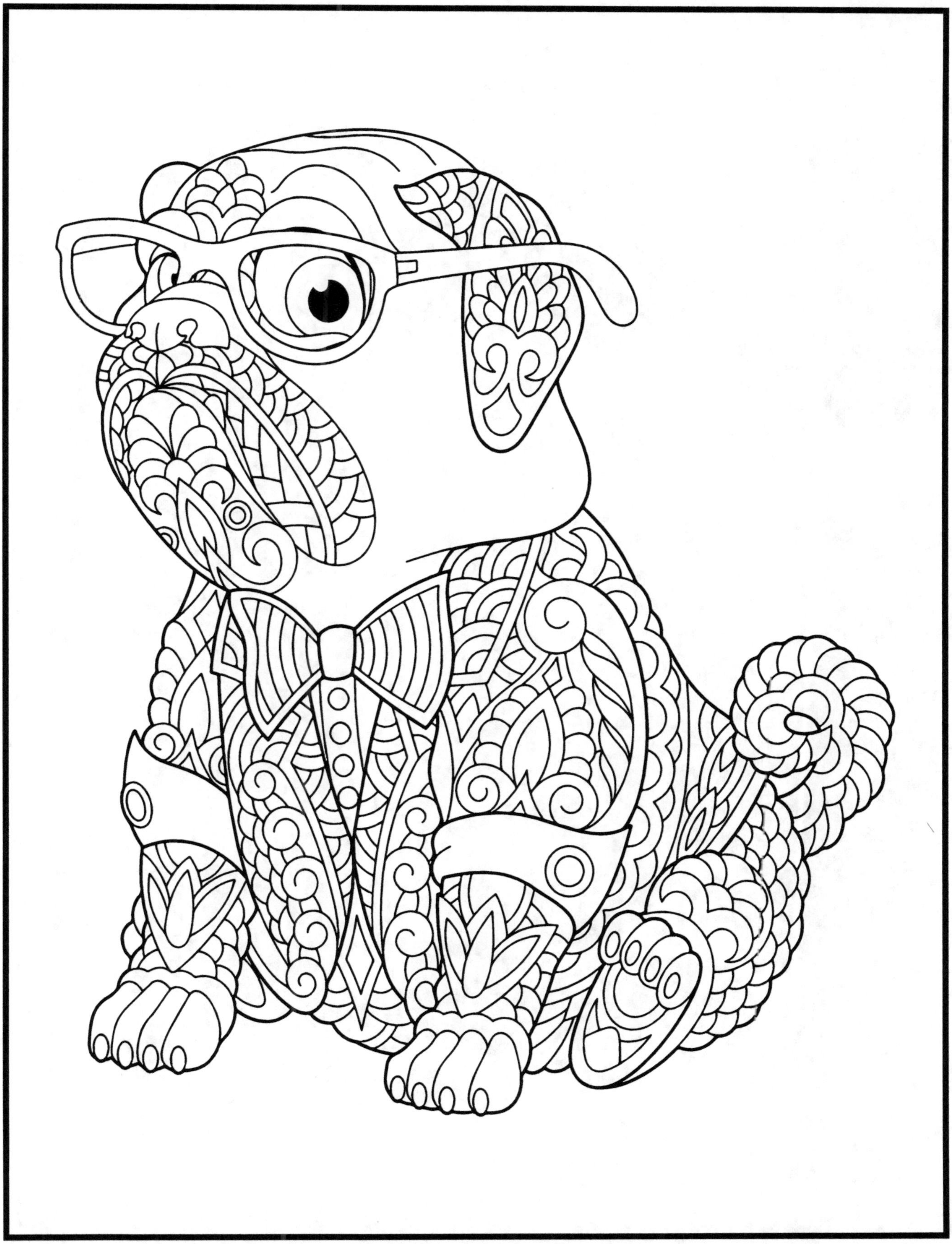

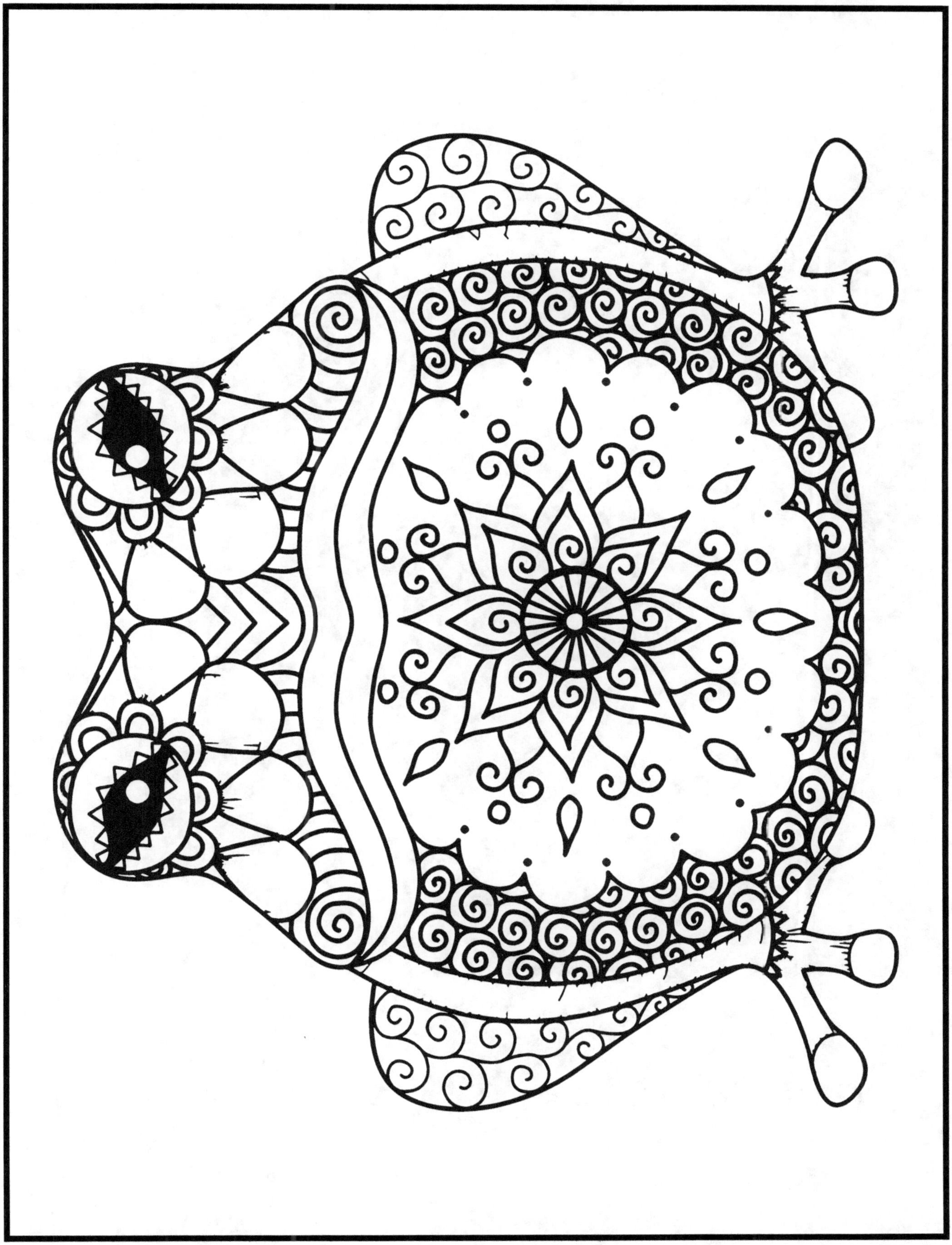

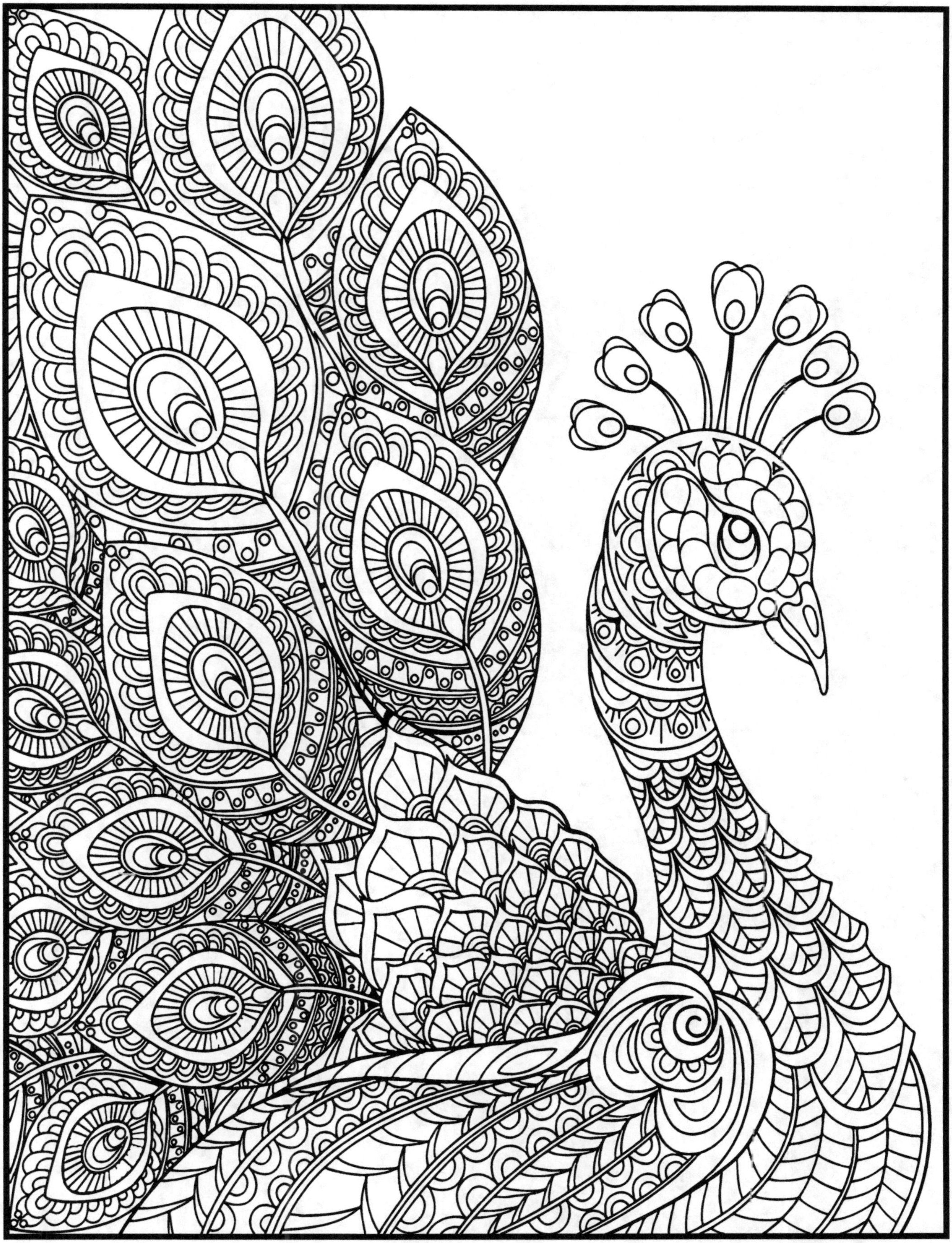

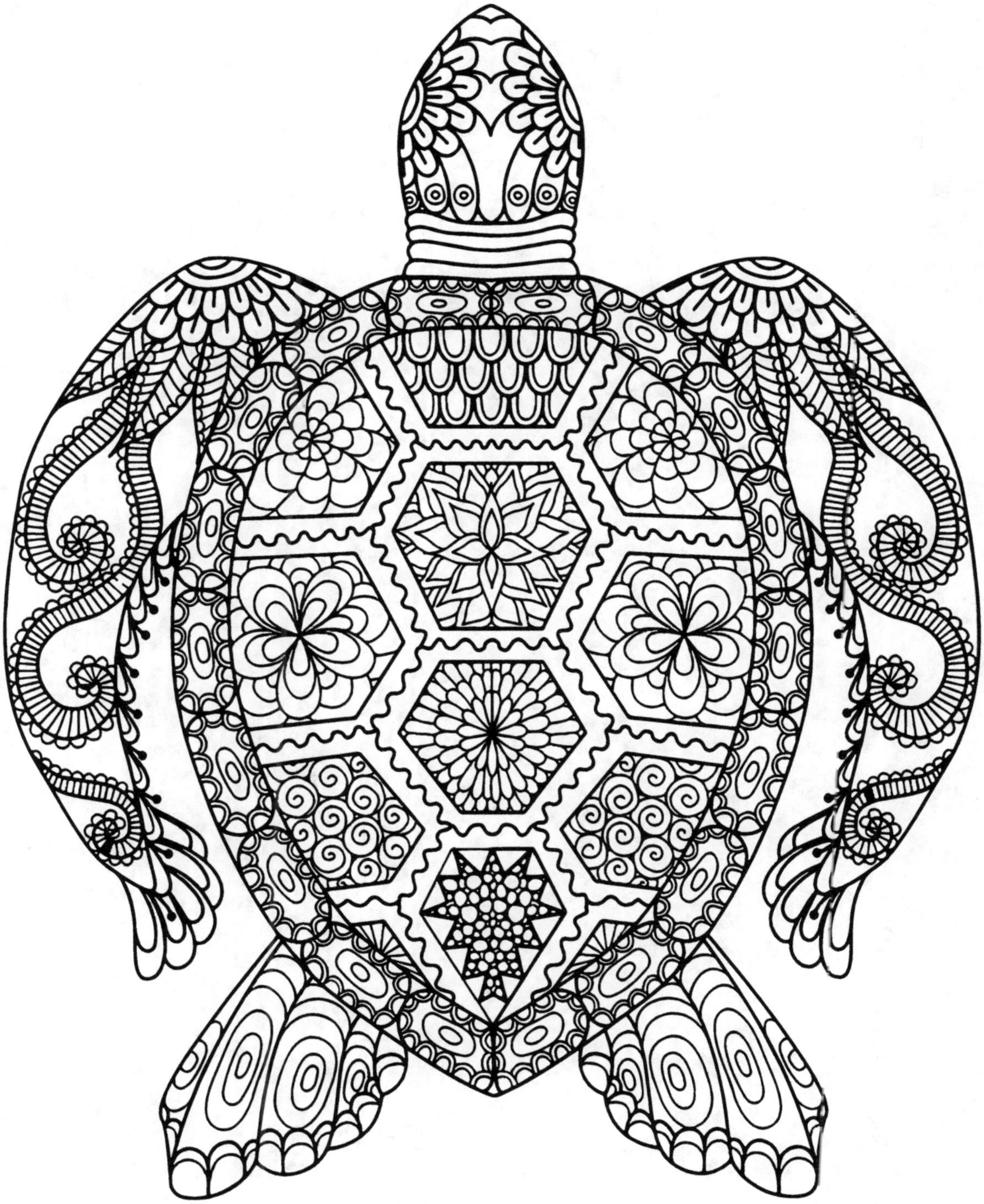

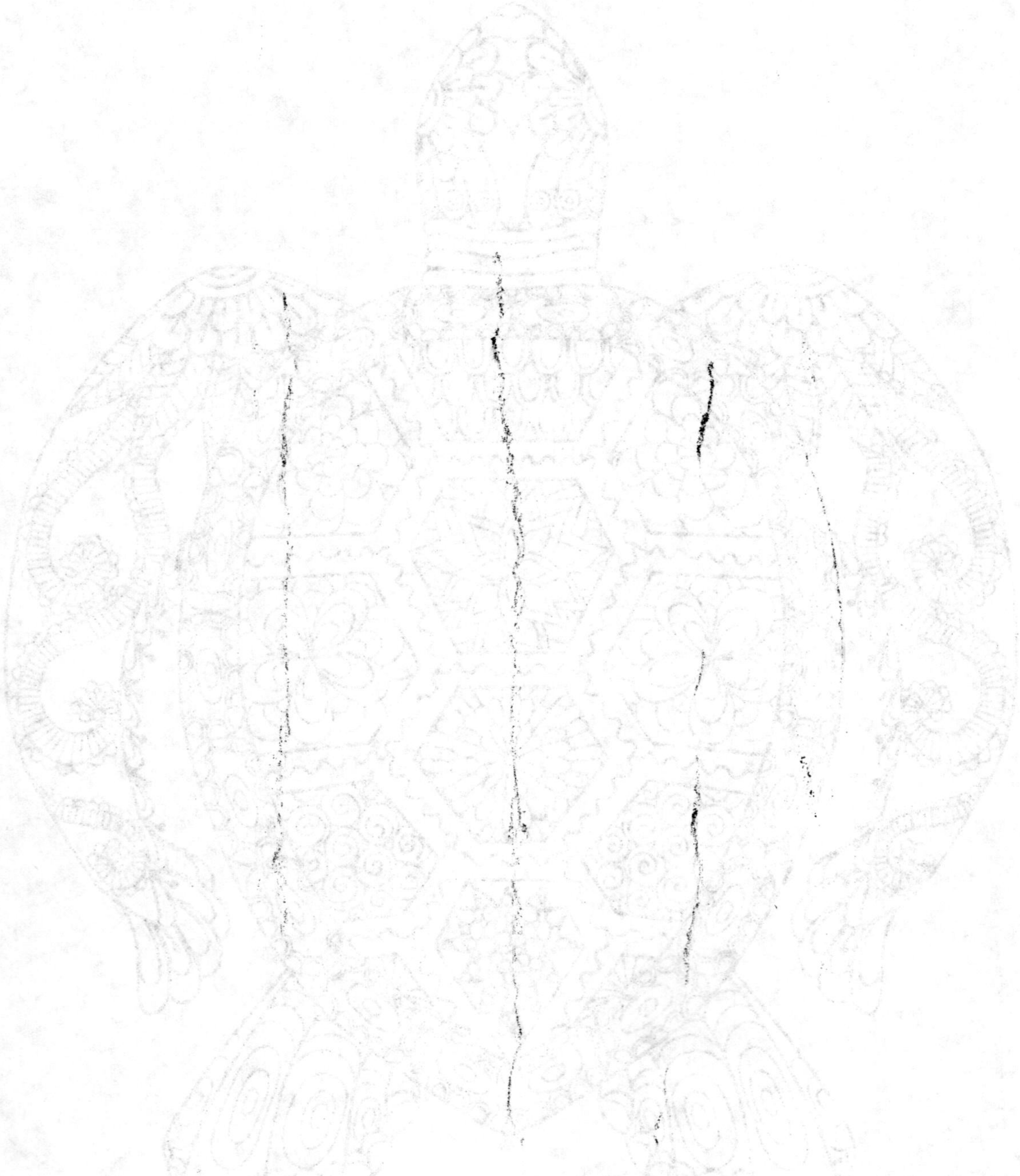

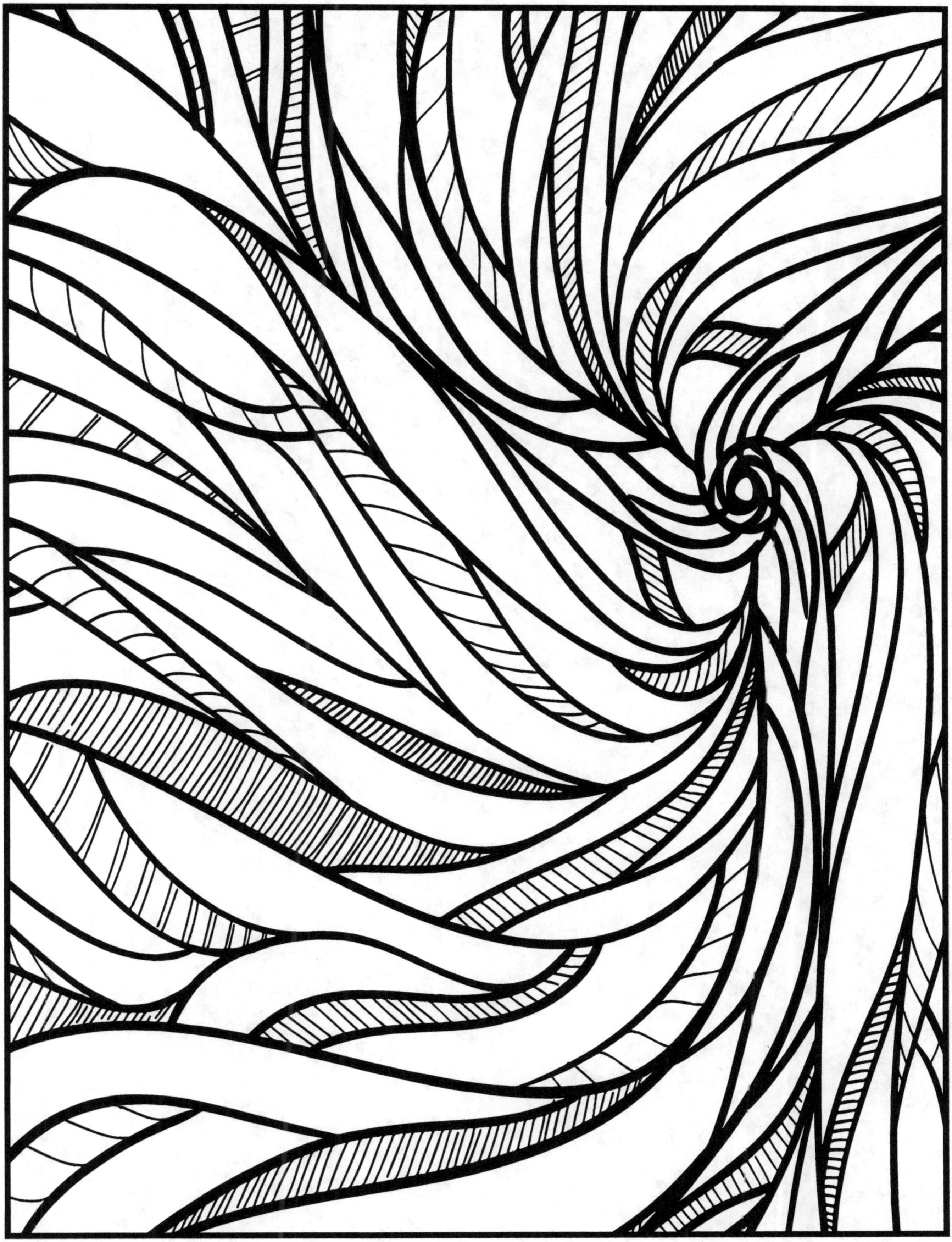

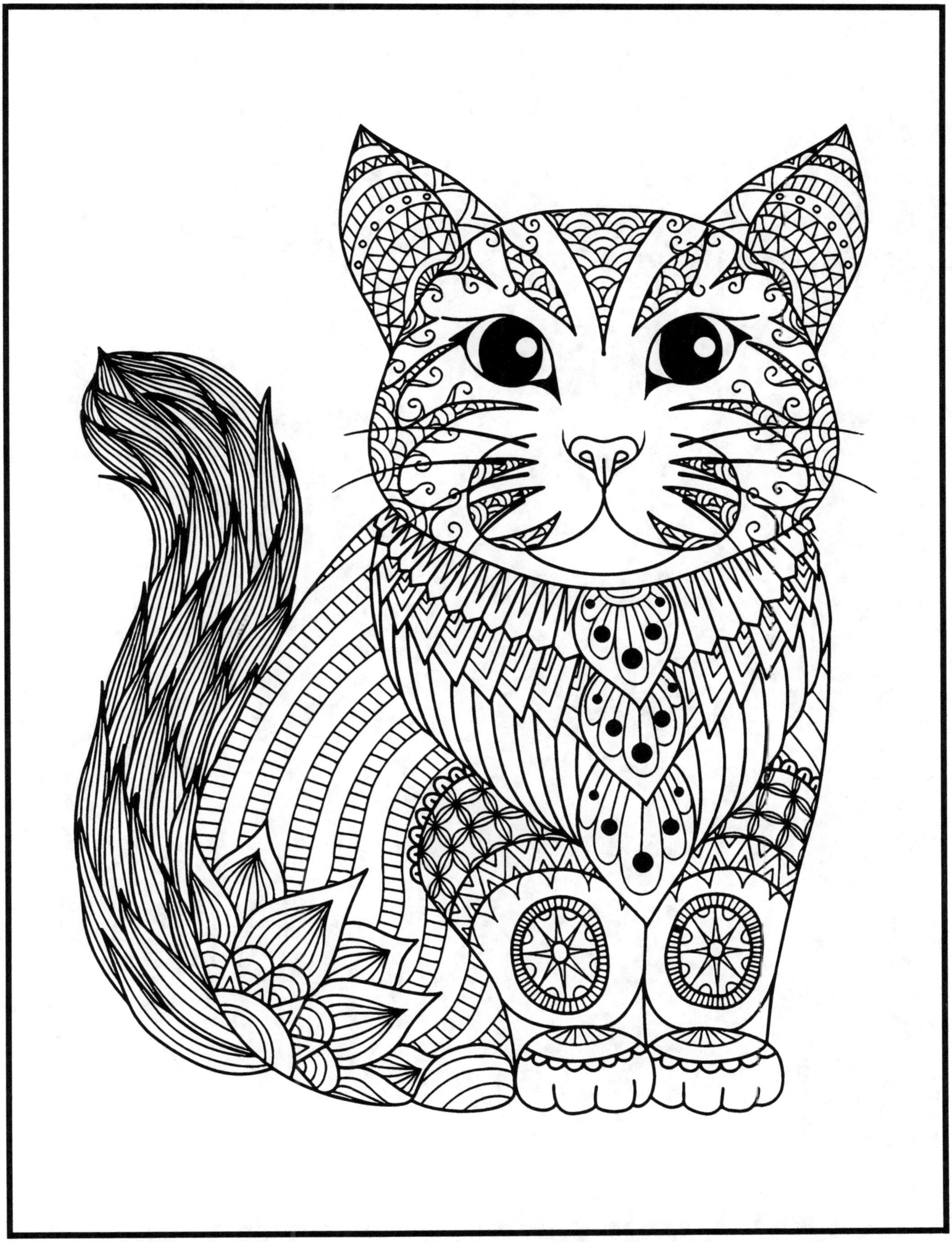

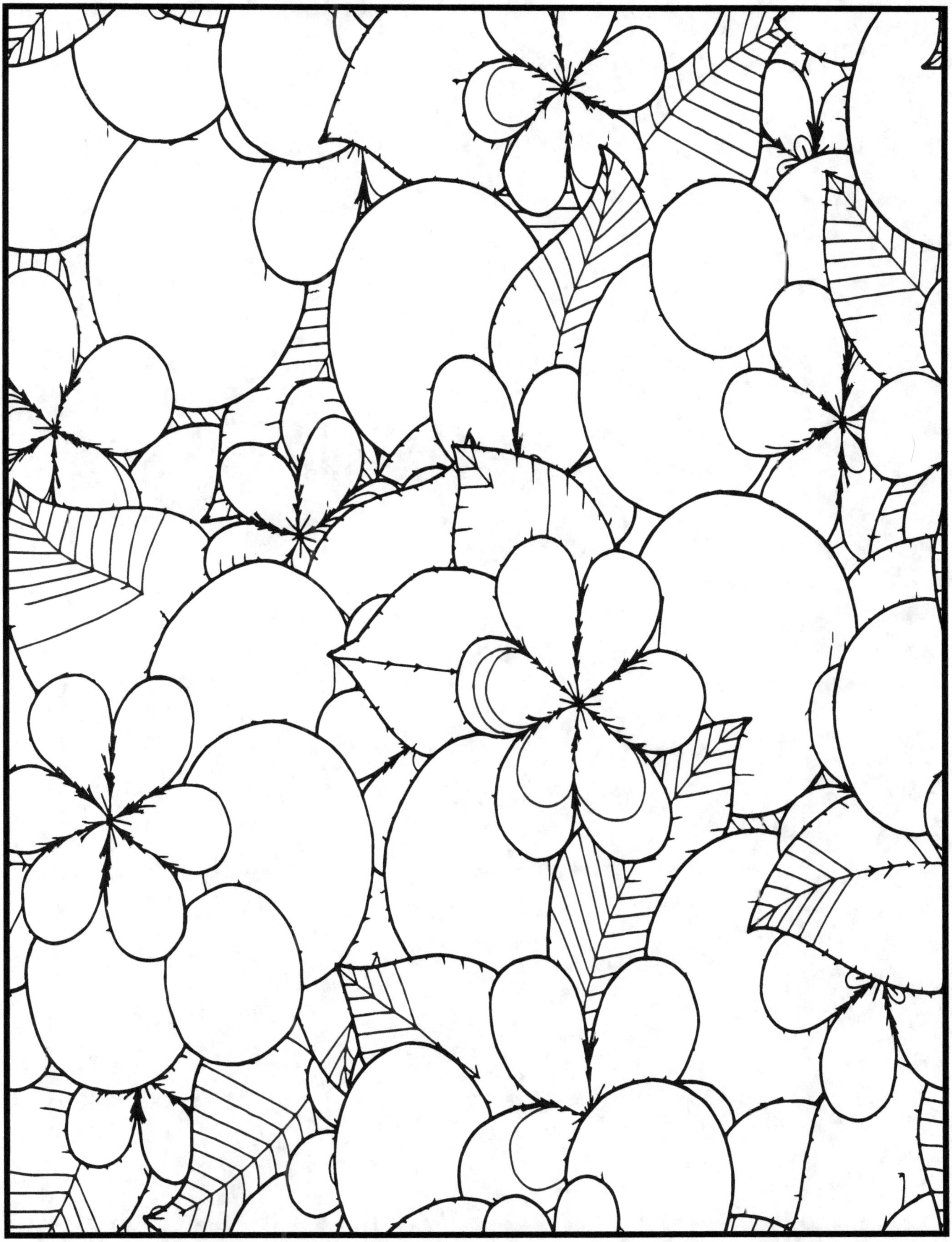

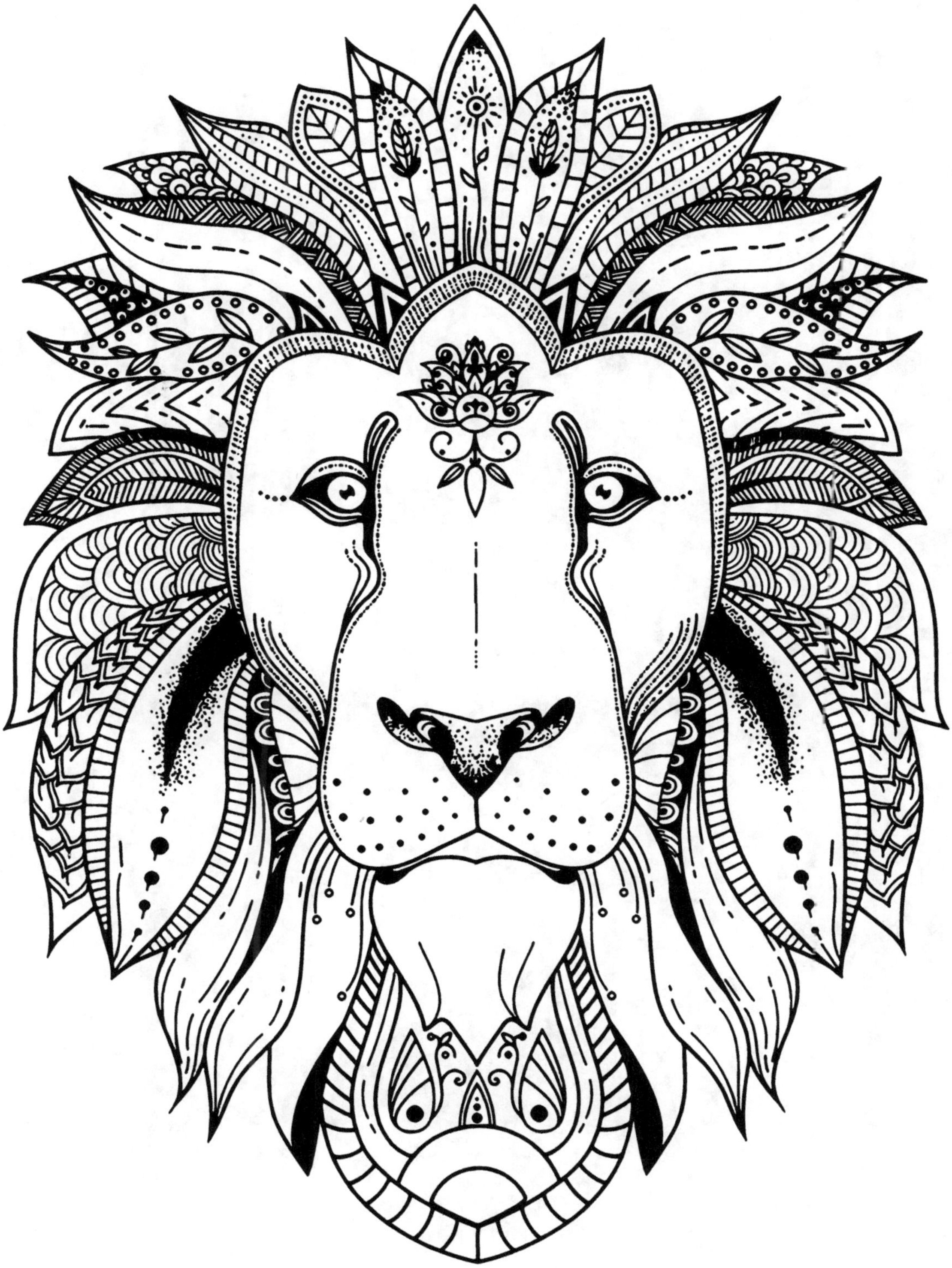

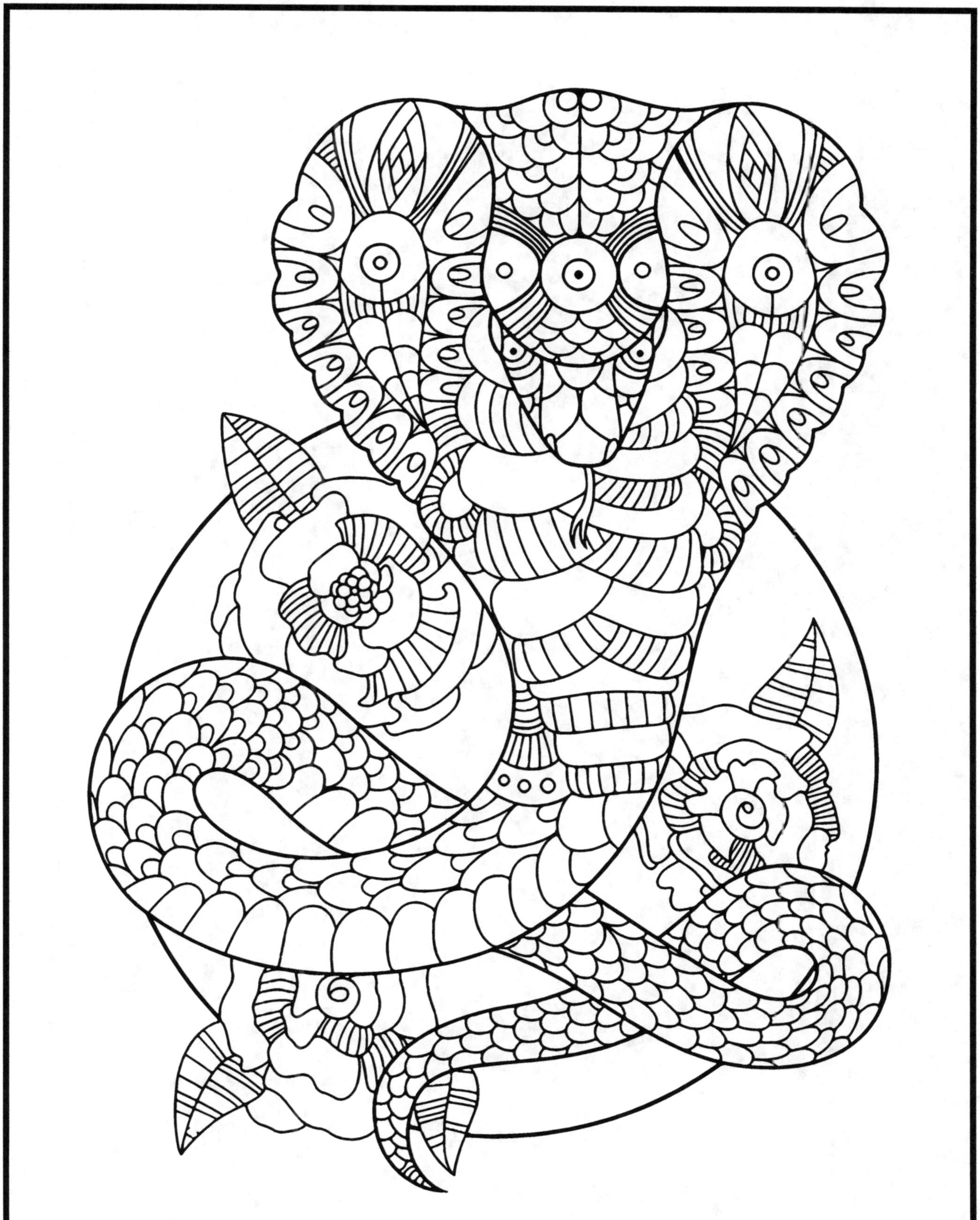

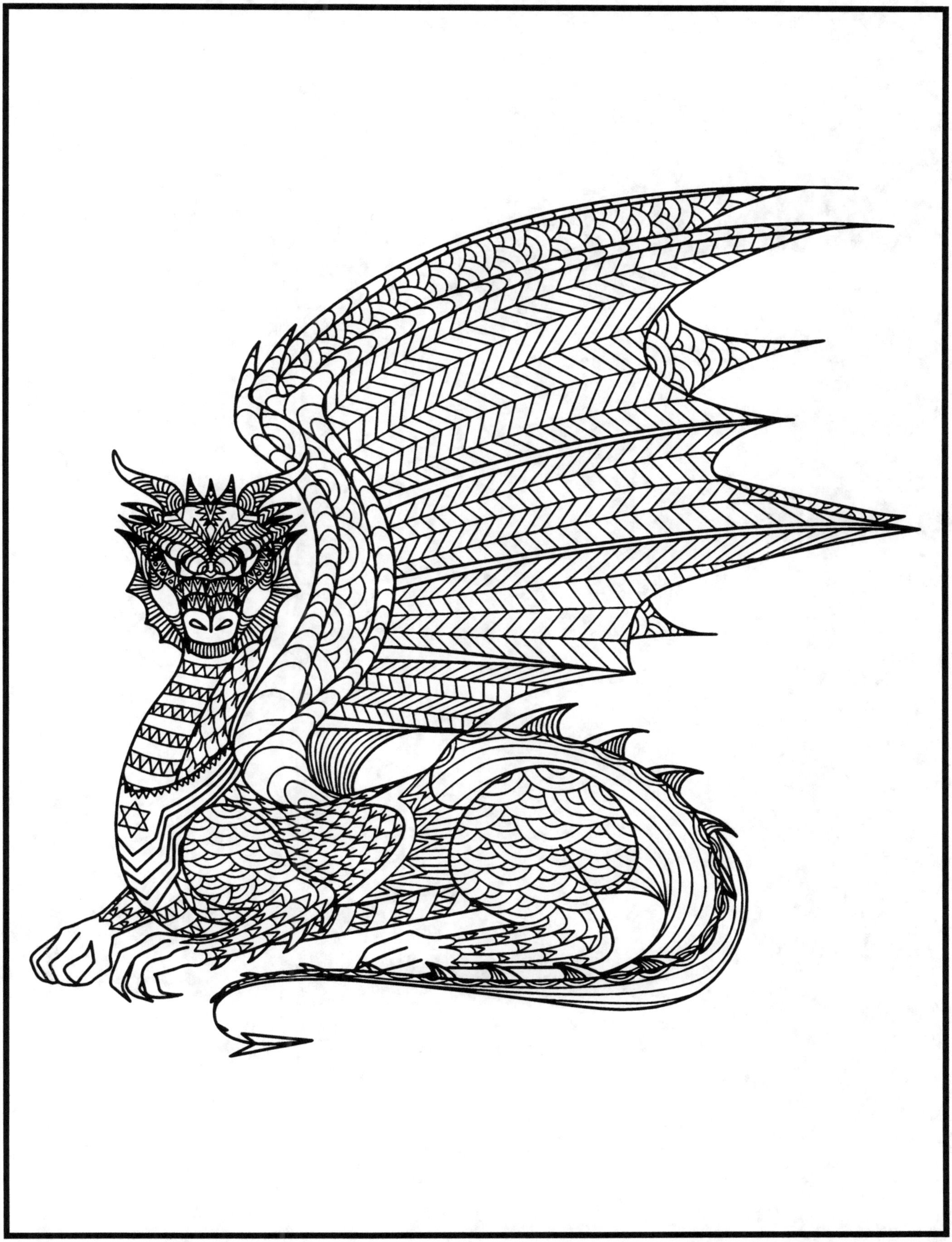

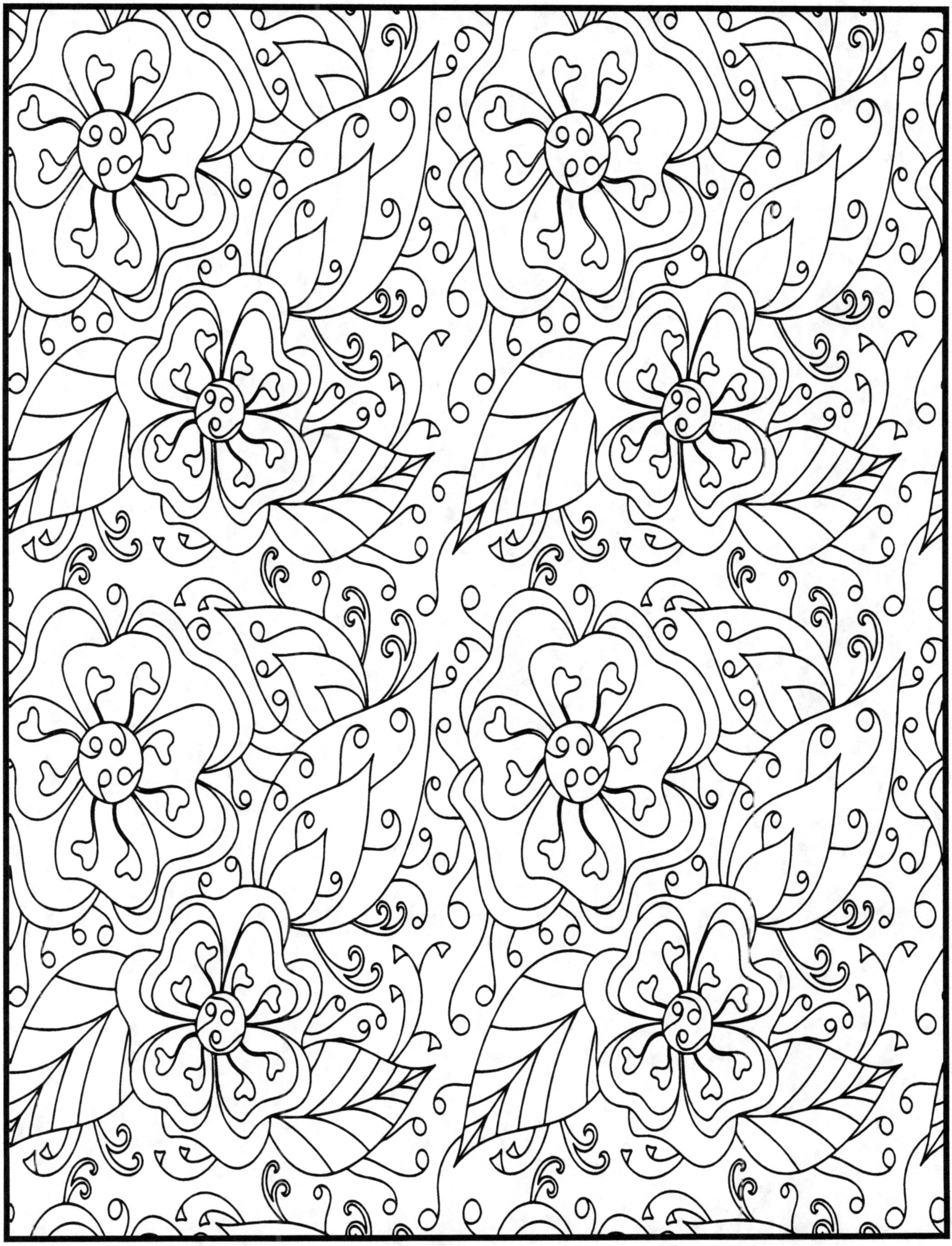

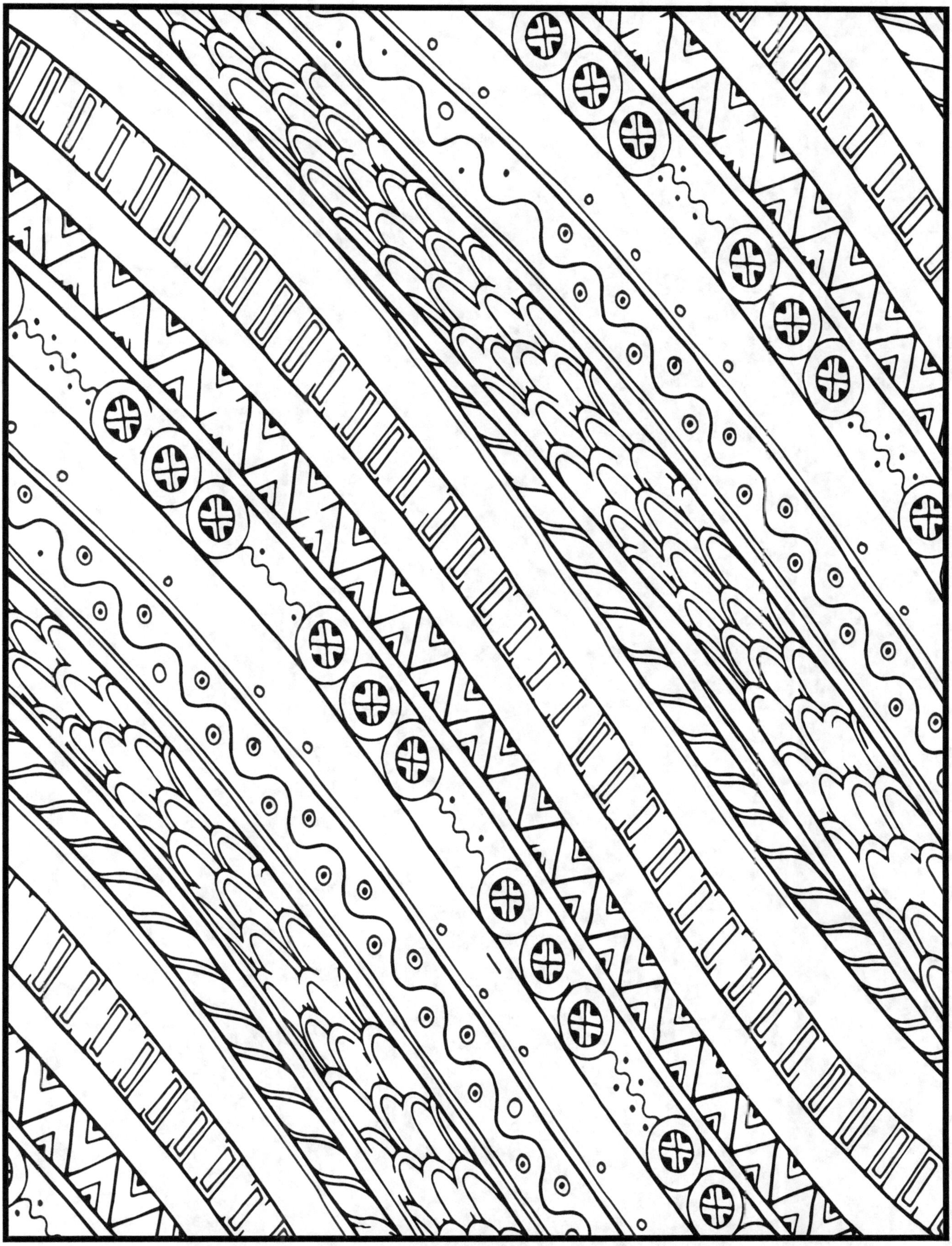

www.ingramcontent.com/pod-product-compliance
Lightning Source LLC
Chambersburg PA
CBHW080554220526
45466CB00010B/3150
* 9 7 9 8 5 9 3 2 6 0 5 4 3 *